Vanessa-Ann's
PLAIN & FANCY CROCHET

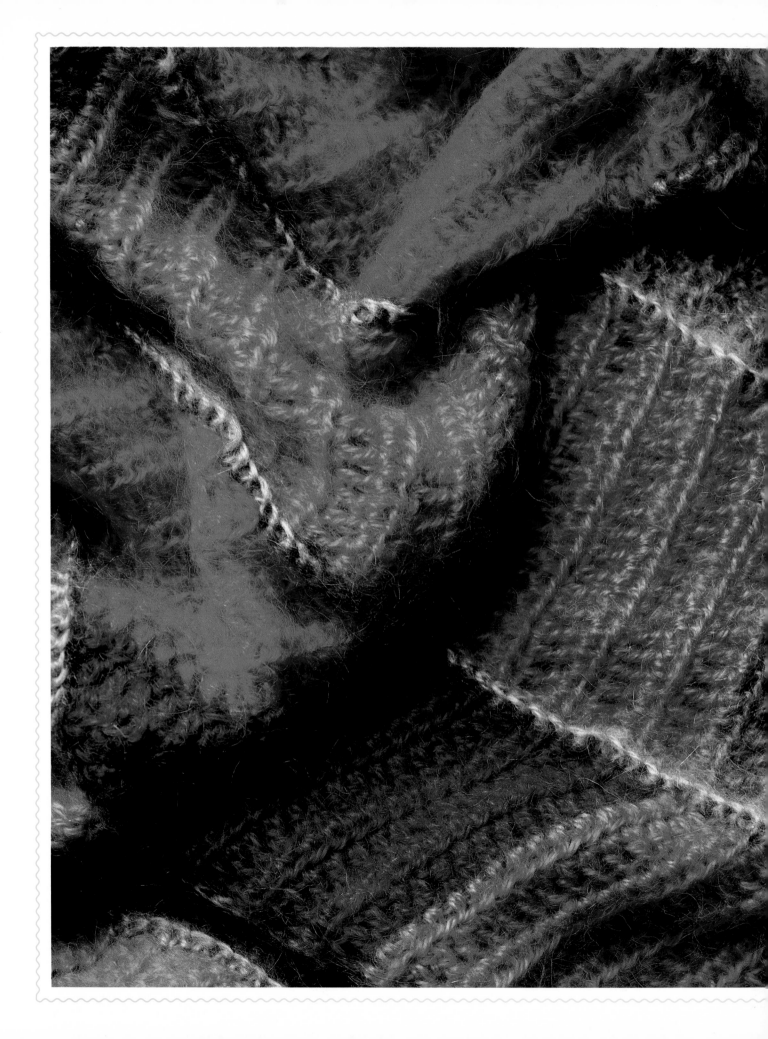

Vanessa - Ann's

PLAIN & FANCY CROCHET

Oxmoor House

To NKW, our fairy godmother,
    With silver threads and golden needles, with patience and understanding, with love and diligence—and a little bit of magic—you have transformed this book into diamonds and emeralds and pearls.

Jo and Tece

For The Vanessa-Ann Collection
Owners: Jo Packham and Terrece Beesley
Designers: Carrie Allen, Terrece Beesley, Marlene Lund, Jo Packham, Jerri Smith
Administrative Staff: Gloria Zirkel Baur, Barbara Milburn, Lisa Miles, Pam Randall
Editorial Staff: Kathi Allred, Trice Boerens, Sandra D. Chapman, Susan Jorgensen, Margaret Shields Marti, Caryol Patterson, Reva Smith Petersen, Florence Stacey, Nancy Whitley

Photographer: Ryne Hazen

The Vanessa-Ann Collection is grateful to the following for sharing their homes and hearths with us: Susan Bingham, Eden, Utah; Mary Gaskill of Trends & Traditions, Ogden, Utah; The Beehive House, home of Brigham Young, second president of the Church of Jesus Christ of Latter Day Saints, Salt Lake City, Utah; and Susan Whitelock, Ogden, Utah.

Vanessa-Ann's Plain & Fancy Crochet
from the *Crochet Treasury* series

©1991 by Oxmoor House, Inc.
Book Division of Southern Progress Corporation
P.O. Box 2463, Birmingham, AL 35201

Library of Congress Catalog Number: 91-62017
ISBN: 0-8487-1063-0
Manufactured in the United States of America
First Printing

Executive Editor: Nancy J. Fitzpatrick
Director of Manufacturing: Jerry Higdon
Art Director: Bob Nance
Copy Chief: Mary Jean Haddin

Editor: Margaret Allen Northen
Editorial Assistant: Catherine S. Corbett
Assistant Copy Editor: Susan Smith Cheatham
Production Manager: Rick Litton
Associate Production Manager: Theresa L. Beste
Production Assistant: Pam Beasley Bullock
Crochet Stitch Illustrations: Barbara Ball

Contents

Town & Country

*Everyone needs an afghan
or two. Whether your home is a
high-rise apartment
in the city or a cozy cottage
in the heart of rural America,
a soft afghan brings warmth
and comfort to your life.
This chapter displays afghans
for every style and taste.
Crochet one or more
to embellish your home.*

Blue Blanket

Pictured on preceding pages.

Finished Size

Approximately 38" x 58", not including edging.

Materials

Sportweight cotton (115-yd. ball): 15 blue, 4 white.

Size G crochet hook, or size to obtain gauge.

Gauge

4 dc and 2 rows = 1".
Cl, 4 dc, cl = 2¼".

Directions

Row 1: With blue, ch 131, dc in 4th ch from hook, dc in next st, [ch 1, sk 1 st, keeping last lp of ea st on hook, work 3 dc in next st, yo and pull through all lps on hook (cl made), ch 1, sk 1 st, dc in ea of next 5 sts] 15 times, ch 1, sk 1 st, cl in next st, ch 1, sk 1 st, dc in ea of next 3 sts, ch 3, turn.

Row 2: Dc in ea of next 2 dc, * cl in next ch-1 sp, ch 1, cl in next ch-1 sp, dc in ea of next 5 dc, rep from * across, end with dc in ea rem st, ch 3, turn.

Row 3: Dc in ea of next 2 dc, * ch 1, sk cl, cl in next ch-1 sp, ch 1, sk cl, dc in ea of next 5 dc, rep from * across, end with dc in ea rem st, ch 3, turn.

Row 4: Rep row 2. Fasten off.

Row 5: Join white, ch 3, rep row 3.

Rows 6 and 7: Rep rows 2 and 3. Fasten off after row 7.

Rows 8-88: Join blue, ch 3, rep rows 2 and 3 alternately. Fasten off after row 88.

Row 89: Join white, ch 3, rep row 3.

Rows 90 and 91: Rep rows 2 and 3. Fasten off after row 91.

Rows 92-95: Join blue, rep rows 2 and 3 alternately. Do not fasten off.

Edging: Rnd 1: Ch 3 for first dc, 4 dc in same st for corner, * 2 dc in end of ea row to next corner, 5 dc in corner, dc in ea st to next corner, 5 dc in corner, rep from * around, end with sl st in top of beg ch-3.

Rnd 2: Ch 6 for first sc and ch 5, sk corner grp, sc bet next 2 sts, [ch 5, sk 3 sts, sc bet next 2 sts], * (ch 5, sk 4 sts, sc bet next 2 sts) to 3 sts before next corner grp, rep bet [ ] once, ch 5, sk corner grp, sc bet next 2 sts, rep from * once more, rep bet [ ] once, cont around as est, end with ch 5, sl st in first ch of beg ch-6.

Rnd 3: Sc in same st, * ch 3, 5 dc in center st of next ch-5 sp, ch 3, sc in next sc, rep from * around, end with sl st in first sc.

Rnd 4: Sl st into ch-3 sp, ch 1, * insert hook from front to back under ch-3 before 5-dc grp, bring hook to front of work under ch-3 after 5-dc grp, work 1 sc (pulls 5-dc grp tog to form a puff), ch 5, rep from * around, end with sl st in beg ch-1.

Rnd 5: Ch 3 for first dc, 2 dc in same st, * 3 dc in ea ch-5 sp to next corner, 6 dc in corner sc, rep from * around, end with 3 dc in beg corner, sl st in top of beg ch-3.

Rnd 6: Ch 5 for first dc and ch 2, dc in same st, ch 2, dc bet last 2 sts of 6-dc grp, ch 2, sk 2 sts, (dc bet next 2 sts, ch 2, sk 2 sts) to next 6-dc corner grp, * dc bet first 2 sts of corner grp, ch 2, sk 2 sts, (dc, ch 2, dc) bet next 2 sts, (ch 2, sk 2 sts, dc bet next 2 sts) to next corner grp, ch 2, rep from * around, end with sl st in 3rd ch of beg ch-5.

Rnd 7: Sl st into ch-2 sp, ch 5 for first dc and ch 2, dc in same sp, * (ch 2, dc in next ch-2 sp) to next corner sp, ch 2, (dc, ch 2, dc) in corner ch-2 sp, rep from * around, sl st in 3rd ch of beg ch-5.

Rnd 8: Rep rnd 7. Fasten off.

Rnd 9: Join white with sl st in any corner ch-2 sp, ch 3 for first dc, (2 dc, ch 3, 3 dc) in same sp for beg corner shell, * ch 3, 2 dc in next sp, ch 3, work a shell of (3 dc, ch 3, 3 dc) in next sp, rep from * around, sl st in top of beg ch-3. Fasten off.

Rnd 10: Join blue with sl st in ch-3 sp before

corner shell, ch 1, * insert hook from front to back under ch-3 before shell, bring hook to front of work under ch-3 after shell, work 1 sc (pulls shell into a puff), ch 5, sk 2 dc, rep from * around, end with sl st in beg ch-1. Fasten off.

Rnd 11: Join blue with sc in sp of rnd-9 corner shell, ch 3 for first dc, (2 dc, ch 3, 3 dc) in same sp for beg corner shell, ch 3, * [working over rnd-10 ch-5 lp, dc in ea of next 2 dc on rnd 9, ch 3, shell in sp of next rnd-9 shell, ch 3] to next corner shell, (shell, ch 3, shell) in sp of corner shell, ch 3, rep from * around, end with 1 shell in beg corner, ch 3, sl st in top of beg ch-3.

Rnd 12: Ch 1, * pull ea shell into a puff by working 1 sc around shell as est, ch 5, rep from * around, end with sl st in first sc.

Rnd 13: Sl st into sp of next shell, ch 3 for first dc, work beg shell as est, * (ch 3, working over rnd-12 ch-5 lp, dc in ea of next 2 dc on rnd 11, ch 3, shell in sp of next shell) to corner, ch 3, shell in first corner shell, ch 3, 2 dc in ch-5 lp (corner inc made), ch 3, shell in next corner shell, rep from * around, sl st in top of beg ch-3.

Rnd 14: Ch 1, * (sc as est to pull ea shell into a puff, ch 5) to 2-dc grp in corner, ch 3, shell bet sts of 2-dc grp, ch 3, rep from * around, end with sl st in first sc.

Rnd 15: Sl st into sp of next shell, ch 3 for first dc, work beg shell as est, * ch 3, working over rnd-14 ch-5 lp, dc in ea of next 2 dc on rnd 13, ch 3, shell in next shell) to corner, ch 3, shell in first corner shell, ch 3, 2 dc in next ch-5 lp, ch 3, sc as est to pull center corner shell into a puff, ch 3, 2 dc in ch-5 lp, rep from * around, end with sl st in top of beg ch-3.

Rnd 16: Ch 1, * (sc as est to pull ea shell into a puff, ch 5) to corner, ch 3, dc in ea of next 2 dc, ch 3, shell in next shell, ch 3, dc in ea of next 2 dc, ch 3, rep from * around, end with sl st in first sc.

Rnd 17: Sl st into sp of next shell, ch 3 for first dc, work beg shell as est, * ch 3, working over rnd-16 ch-5 lp, dc in ea of next 2 dc on rnd 15, ch 3, shell in next shell) to corner, ch 3, shell in first corner shell, ch 3, dc in ea of next 2 dc, ch 3, sc as est to pull center corner shell into a puff, ch 3, dc in ea of next 2 dc, rep from * around, end with sl st in top of beg ch-3.

Rnds 18 and 19: Rep rnds 16 and 17. Fasten off after rnd 19.

Jewel Tones

Finished Size

Approximately 50" x 70", not including fringe.

Materials

Worsted-weight acrylic-mohair blend (185-yd. ball): 7 turquoise (A), 1 forest green (B), 5 peacock blue (C), 1 dark purple (D), 3 dark blue (E), 1 medium blue (F), 3 fuchsia (G), 1 green (H), 1 magenta (I).

Size I crochet hook, or size to obtain gauge.

Gauge

1 section = 5" x 7".

Directions

Note: Refer to placement diagram for colors used to make ea panel.

Panels 1, 3, 5, 7, and 9: Section 1: With first color, ch 18.

Row 1: Hdc in 3rd ch from hook and ea ch across, turn = 17 sts (including beg ch-2).

Row 2: Ch 3 for first dc, dc in same st as tch and ea of next 13 sts, keeping last lp of ea st on hook, dc in last st and tch, yo and pull through all lps on hook (dec made over last st and tch), turn = 16 sts.

Row 3: Ch 2 for first hdc, hdc in same st as tch and ea st across, turn = 17 sts.

Row 4: Ch 3 for first dc, dc in same st as tch and ea of next 13 sts, dec over last st and tch, turn = 16 sts.

Rows 5-14: Rep rows 3 and 4 alternately. Fasten off.

Section 2: With right side facing, join 2nd color with sl st in corner.

Rows 1-14: Rep rows 3 and 4 alternately as est in first section. Fasten off.

Section 3: With right side facing, join 3rd color with sl st in corner.

Rows 1-14: Rep rows 3 and 4 alternately as est in first section. Fasten off.

Rep sections 1-3 twice more, working colors as indicated on placement diagram. Rep section 1 once more to complete panel.

Panels 2, 4, 6, 8, and 10: Section 1: With first color, ch 18.

Row 1: Hdc in 3rd ch from hook and ea ch across, turn = 17 sts (including beg ch-2).

Row 2: Ch 3 for first dc, dc in ea of 14 sts, 2 dc in last st, turn = 17 sts.

Row 3: Ch 2 for first hdc, hdc in same st as tch and ea st across, turn.

Row 4: Ch 3 for first dc, dc in ea of 14 sts, 2 dc in last st, turn.

Rows 5-14: Rep rows 3 and 4 alternately. Fasten off.

Section 2: With right side facing, join 2nd color with sl st in corner.

Rows 1-14: Rep rows 3 and 4 alternately as est in first section. Fasten off.

Sections		1	2	3	4	5	6	7	8	9	10
	1	C	E	B	A	C	G	A	C	D	A
	3	H	A	G	C	F	D	C	G	E	B
	2	A	C	A	I	G	I	G	H	F	C
	1	C	E	B	A	C	G	A	C	D	A
	3	H	A	G	C	F	D	C	G	E	B
	2	A	C	A	I	G	I	G	H	F	C
	1	C	E	B	A	C	G	A	C	D	A
	3	H	A	G	C	F	D	C	G	E	C
	2	A	C	A	I	G	I	G	H	F	B
	1	C	E	B	A	C	G	A	C	D	A

1 2 3 4 5 6 7 8 9 10

Panels

Placement Diagram

Section 3: With right side facing, join 3rd color with sl st in corner.

Rows 1-14: Rep rows 3 and 4 alternately as est in first section. Fasten off.

Rep sections 1-3 twice more, working colors as indicated on placement diagram. Rep section 1 once more to complete panel.

Assembly: Referring to diagram for placement, holding first 2 panels with wrong sides facing and working through both pieces, join turquoise with sl st in corner, sc in ea st across, matching section edges. Fasten off. Rep to join rem panels.

Edging: Rnd 1: With right side facing and afghan turned to work across long edge, join turquoise with sl st in corner, ch 1, 2 sc in same corner, * hdc in ea st to corner, 3 sc in corner, hdc in ea st to joining of 2 panels, [pull up a lp in last st of first panel, pull up a lp in first st of next panel, yo and pull through all lps on hook (dec made at inside point), hdc in ea st to next inside point] to next corner, 3 sc in corner, rep from * around, sc in beg corner, sl st in first sc.

Rnd 2: Ch 1, working in bk lps only, 3 sc in center corner st, * sc in ea st to corner, 3 sc in corner, (sc in ea st to inside point, dec at inside point as est) to next corner st, 3 sc in corner st, rep from * around, sl st in first sc.

Rnds 3 and 4: Rep rnds 1 and 2.

Rnd 5: Sl st into center corner st, ch 2 for first hdc, 2 hdc in same corner st, * hdc in ea st to corner, 3 hdc in corner, (hdc in ea st to inside point, dec at inside point as est, hdc in ea st to outside point, 3 hdc in st at outside point) to next corner, 3 hdc in corner st, rep from * around, sl st in top of beg ch-2.

Rnd 6: Ch 1, (sl st, ch 1, sl st) in corner st, * sl st in ea st to next corner, (sl st, ch 1, sl st) in corner st, [sl st in ea st to inside point, sk 1 st at inside point, sl st in ea st to outside point, (sl st, ch 1, sl st) in st at outside point] to next corner, (sl st, ch 1, sl st) in corner st, rep from * around. Fasten off.

Fringe: For each tassel, cut 18 (29") strands of yarn, using colors as desired. Knot 31 tassels evenly spaced across each short edge of afghan.

Grapevine

Grapevine

Finished Size

Approximately 58" x 70".

Materials

Worsted-weight acrylic-wool blend (200-yd. skein): 15 tan.

Size G crochet hook, or size to obtain gauge.

Worsted-weight acrylic (230-yd. skein): 1 each light green, dark plum, plum, cranberry, medium rose, light rose.

Sizes #1, #5, and #6 steel crochet hooks.

Stuffing.

Gauge

6 hdc and 5 rows = 2" with size G hook.

Directions

Center panel (make 1): With size G hook and tan, ch 122.

Row 1: Hdc in 3rd ch from hook and ea ch across, ch 2, turn.

Row 2: Hdc in ea st across, ch 2, turn = 120 hdc.

Rows 3-134: Rep row 2. Do not fasten off after last row. Work * 3 sc in corner, sc in ea st to next corner, rep from * around, sl st in first sc. Fasten off.

Side panel (make 2): With tan, ch 31.

Row 1: Hdc in 3rd ch from hook and ea ch across, ch 2, turn = 29 hdc.

Rows 2-4: Hdc in ea st across, ch 2, turn.
Note: To make a tr tr, yo 4 times.

Row 5: Hdc in ea of next 4 sts, tr tr around post of 6th hdc on row 1, sk hdc behind tr tr just made, hdc in ea of next 4 sts, tr tr around post of 9th hdc from last tr tr, sk hdc behind tr tr just made, hdc in ea of next 3 sts, (yo and pull up a lp in next st) 7 times, yo and pull through all lps on hook, ch 1 (puff made), hdc in ea of next 3 sts, tr tr around same post as last tr tr, sk hdc behind tr tr just made, hdc in ea of next 4 sts, tr tr around post of 9th hdc from last tr tr, sk hdc behind tr tr just made, hdc in ea of next 4 sts and in tch, ch 2, turn.

Row 6: Hdc in ea st across, sk ch-1 of ea puff = 29 hdc, ch 2, turn.

Rows 7 and 8: Hdc in ea st across, ch 2, turn.

Row 9: Hdc in ea of next 4 sts, tr tr in top of first row-5 tr tr, sk hdc behind tr tr just made, hdc in ea of next 8 sts, keeping last lp of ea st on hook, tr tr in top of ea of next 2 row-5 tr tr, yo and pull through all lps on hook (top point of diamond made), sk hdc behind tr tr just made, hdc in ea of next 8 sts, tr tr in top of last row-5 tr tr, sk hdc behind tr tr just made, hdc in ea of next 4 sts and in tch, ch 2, turn.

Rows 10-12: Hdc in ea st across, ch 2, turn (diamond pat est).

Row 13: Rep row 5, working first tr tr through top of first row-9 tr tr, 2nd and 3rd tr tr through top point of diamond made in row 9, and last tr tr through top of last row-9 tr tr.

Rep rows 5-12 of pat for a total of 164 rows, end with 1 rep of rows 5-9 to finish last diamond = 169 rows and 21 diamonds. Do not fasten off after last row. Work * 3 sc in corner, sc in ea st to next corner, rep from * around, sl st in first sc. Fasten off.

End panel (make 2): With tan, ch 122.

Row 1: Hdc in 3rd ch from hook and ea ch across, ch 2, turn = 120 hdc.

Rows 2 and 3: Hdc in ea st across, ch 2, turn.

Row 4: Hdc in ea of next 4 sts, tr tr around post of 6th hdc on row 1, * sk hdc behind tr tr just made, hdc in ea of next 4 sts, tr tr around post of 9th hdc from last tr tr, sk hdc behind tr tr just made, hdc in ea of next 3 sts, puff in next st, hdc in ea of next 3 sts, tr tr around post of same st as last tr tr, sk hdc behind tr tr just made, hdc in ea of next 4 sts, tr tr around post of 9th hdc from last tr tr, sk hdc behind tr tr just made **, hdc in ea of next 11 sts, tr tr around post of 12th hdc from last tr tr, rep from * to **, hdc in ea of next 12 sts, tr tr around post of 13th hdc from last tr tr, rep from * to **, hdc in ea of next 11 sts, tr tr around post of 12th hdc from last tr tr, rep from * to **, end with hdc in ea of next 4 sts and in tch, ch 2, turn.

Row 5: Hdc in ea st across, sk ch-1 of ea puff, ch 2, turn = 120 hdc.

Rows 6 and 7: Hdc in ea st across, ch 2, turn.

Row 8: Hdc in ea of next 4 sts, tr tr in top of first row-4 tr tr, * sk hdc behind tr tr just made, hdc in ea of next 8 hdc, keeping last lp of ea st on hook, tr tr in top of ea of next 2 row-4 tr tr, yo and pull through all lps on hook (top point of diamond made), sk hdc behind tr tr just made, hdc in ea of next 8 sts, tr tr in top of next row-4 tr tr **, hdc in ea of next 11 sts, tr tr in top of next tr tr, rep from * to **, hdc in ea of next 12 sts, tr tr in top of next tr tr, rep from * to **, hdc in ea of next 11 sts, tr tr in top of next tr tr, rep from * to **, end with hdc in ea of 4 sts and in tch, ch 2, turn.

Rows 9-11: Hdc in ea st across, ch 2, turn.

Rows 12-16: Rep rows 4-8. Do not fasten off after last row. Work * 3 sc in corner, sc in ea st to next corner, rep from * around, sl st in first sc. Fasten off.

Assembly: *Note:* Last row of pat is top edge of ea panel. Holding panels with wrong sides facing and working through both pieces, join top edge of center panel to bottom edge of 1 end panel as foll: join tan in center corner st, (ch 1, sk next st, sl st in next st) across, end with sl st in center corner st. Fasten off. Rep to join top edge of rem end panel to bottom edge of center panel. With top edges aligned, rep to join a side panel to ea side edge.

Small leaf (make 22): **Row 1:** With size #1 hook and light green, ch 10, sc in 2nd ch from hook and ea of next 7 ch, 2 sc in last ch, working across opposite side of ch, sc in ea of next 8 sts, ch 1, turn.

Note: Work in bk lps only for rows 2-4.

Row 2: Sk first sc, sc in ea of next 7 sc, 2 sc in ea of next 2 sc, sc in ea of next 6 sc, ch 1, turn.

Row 3: Sk first sc, sc in ea of next 6 sc, 2 sc in ea of next 2 sc, sc in ea of next 6 sc, ch 1, turn.

Row 4: Sk first sc, sc in ea of next 6 sc, 2 sc in ea of next 2 sc, sc in ea of next 5 sc. Fasten off.

Large leaf (make 11): **Row 1:** With size #1 hook and light green, ch 17, sc in 2nd ch from hook and ea of next 14 ch, 2 sc in last ch, working across opposite side of ch, sc in ea of next 15 sts, ch 1, turn.

Note: Work in bk lps only for rows 2-5.

Row 2: Sk first sc, sc in ea of next 15 sc, 2 sc in ea of next 2 sc, sc in ea of next 14 sc, ch 1, turn.

Row 3: Sk first sc, sc in ea of next 14 sc, 2 sc in ea of next 2 sc, sc in ea of next 14 sc, ch 1, turn.

Row 4: Sk first sc, sc in ea of next 14 sc, 2 sc in ea of next 2 sc, sc in ea of next 13 sc, ch 1, turn.

Row 5: Sk first sc, sc in ea of next 13 sc, 2 sc in ea of next 2 sc, sc in ea of next 13 sc. Fasten off.

Spiral vine (make 10): With size #1 hook and light green, ch 25. Work 3 sc in ea ch. Fasten off.

Grape: Make 28 from dark plum, 76 from plum, 25 from cranberry, 25 from medium rose, 28 from light rose. *Note:* Use size #6 hook to make some of the grapes for a variety of sizes.

With size #5 hook, ch 5, join with a sl st to form a ring.

Rnd 1: Work 6 sc in ring, sl st in first sc.

Rnd 2: Ch 1, 2 sc in ea st around, sl st in beg ch-1.

Rnd 3: Ch 1, (2 sc in next sc, sc in next sc) around, sl st in beg ch-1.

Rnd 4: Ch 1, * sc in ea of next 2 sc, pull up a lp in ea of next 2 sts, yo and pull through all lps (dec made over 2 sc), rep from * around, sl st in beg ch-1.

Rnd 5: Rep rnd 4.

Rnd 6: Put a small amount of stuffing in grape. (Dec over next 2 sts) around. Fasten off, leaving a tail of yarn. Pull tail through middle of grape and out through beg ring.

Finishing: With tan, sew grapes, leaves, and spiral vines to afghan as desired (see photo).

Midnight Rose

Finished Size

Approximately 49" x 65", not including edging.

Materials

Worsted-weight acrylic (110-yd. ball): 32 black.

Size I (14"-long) afghan hook, or size to obtain gauge.

Size G crochet hook.

Paternayan Persian wool (8-yd. skein): see color key (on page 18).

Gauge

8 sts and 7 rows = 2" in afghan st.

Directions

Note: See page 141 for afghan st instructions.

Center panel (make 1): With black, ch 111, work 155 rows afghan st. Sl st in ea vertical bar across. Do not fasten off last lp.

Border: With size G crochet hook, ch 1, work 2 sc in same st, * sc in ea st to next corner, 3 sc in corner, rep from * around, sc in beg corner, sl st in first sc. Fasten off.

Side panel (make 2): With black, ch 44, work 155 rows afghan st. Sl st in ea vertical bar across. Work border as for center panel. Fasten off.

End panel (make 2): With black, ch 111, work 44 rows afghan st. Sl st in ea vertical bar across. Work border as for center panel. Fasten off.

Corner panel (make 4): With black, ch 44, work 44 rows afghan st. Sl st in ea vertical bar across. Work border as for center panel. Fasten off.

Cross-stitch: Charts are on page 19. Stitch design with 2 strands of wool. Center design on panel. With last row of afghan stitch at top, work end panel design on 1 end panel; work mirror image of design on remaining end panel. With last row of afghan stitch at left-hand end, work side panel design on 1 side panel; work mirror image on remaining side panel.

Assembly: Holding 2 panels with wrong sides facing and working through both pieces, join black with sl st in corner, * ch 1, sk next st, sl st in next st, rep from * to next corner. Fasten off. Rep to join all panels.

Edging: Rnd 1: With size G crochet hook, join black with a sl st in any corner, ch 1, 2 sc in same st, * ch 12, sk 8 sts, sc in ea of next 3 sts, ch 12, sk next 9 sts, sc in ea of next 3 sts, rep from * around, sc in beg corner, sl st in first sc. (*Note:* Work center st of 3-sc grp in joining bet panels and 3 sc in ea corner st. Adjust the number of sk sts as necessary to have 4 lps across ea edge of ea corner panel, 10 lps across ea end panel, and 14 lps across ea side panel = 80 lps around afghan.)

Rnd 2: Ch 1, sc in next st, * 15 dc in lp, sc in ea of next 3 sc, rep from * around, end with sc in last sc, sl st in beg ch.

Rnd 3: Ch 1, sc in same st, * ch 3, sk 1 sc and 2 dc, sc in next dc, ch 3, sk 2 dc, 2 dc in ea of next 5 dc, ch 3, sk 2 dc, sc in next dc, ch 3, sc in center st of next 3-sc grp, rep from * around, sl st in first sc.

Rnd 4: Ch 3, sc in next ch-3 sp, * ch 3, sc in next ch-3 sp, ch 3, sk 2 dc, sc in next dc, ch 3, sk 3 dc, 3 dc bet next 2 dc, ch 3, sk 2 dc, sc in next dc, (ch 3, sc in next ch-3 sp) twice, ch 2 **, sl st in next sc, ch 2, sc in next ch-3 sp, rep from * around, end last rep at **, sl st in base of beg ch-3. Fasten off.

Rnd 5: *Note:* Work cl in center st of sp created by ch-12 lps on rnd-1 of edging. Join black in 5th sc from corner on border rnd, ch 4 for first tr, keeping last lp of ea st on hook, work 3 tr in same st, yo and pull through all lps on hook, sl st around post of center st of rnd-2 15-dc grp, * ch 30, sk across to center st of next sp, keeping last lp of ea st on hook, work 4 tr in same st, yo and pull through all lps on hook (4-tr cl made), sl st around post of center st of rnd-2 15-dc grp, rep from * around, end with sl st in top of beg ch-4. Fasten off.

Tassels (make 80): Cut 20 (17") strands for each tassel. Knot a tassel in each chain-30 loop around afghan.

Color Key

Note: The number of 8-yd. skeins required for each color is indicated in parentheses.

Paternayan Persian wool (used for sample)

S	733	Gold (2)
E	497	Beige (2)
·	865	Peach-lt. (6)
−	864	Peach-med. (6)
O	862	Peach-dk. (4)
+	955	Salmon-lt. (6)
△	953	Salmon-med. (3)
H	951	Salmon-dk. (4)
□	933	Rose-lt. (3)
✕	932	Rose-med. (4)
G	930	Rose-dk. (6)
●	922	Pink-med. (3)
▽	912	Mauve (2)
∴	323	Lavender-lt. (2)
▣	321	Lavender-dk. (2)
•	604	Green-lt. (3)
I	603	Green-med. (4)
O	662	Blue Green-med. (12)
✕	661	Blue Green-dk. (14)
▲	484	Mahogany-lt. (2)
∴	872	Mahogany-med. (3)
■	871	Mahogany-dk. (12)
N	870	Mahogany-vy. dk. (3)

18

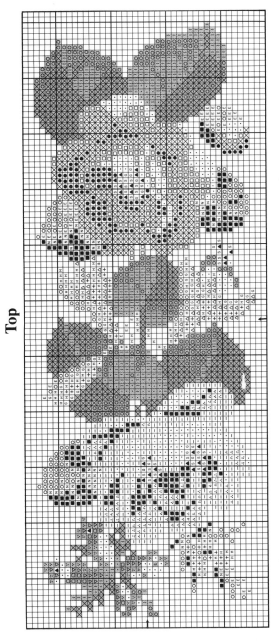

End Panel
Cross-stitch Chart

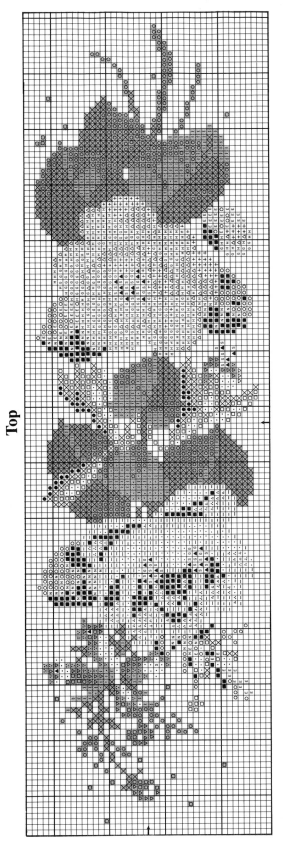

Side Panel
Cross-stitch Chart

Woven Rings

Finished Size

Afghan: Approximately 48" x 80", not including edging.
Pillow: Approximately 15½" square.

Materials

Worsted-weight acrylic (110-yd. ball): 20 gray, 19 blue, 15 green for afghan; 1 each gray, blue, green for pillow.
Size F crochet hook, or size to obtain gauge.
¾ yard of purple polished cotton fabric.
Sewing thread to match fabric.
1¾ yards (½") cording.
16"-square pillow form.

Gauge

Afghan square = 16".
Pillow square = 15".

Directions

Afghan square (make 15): **First ring:** With gray, ch 22, join with a sl st to form a ring. Ch 1, 40 sc in ring, sl st in beg ch-1. Fasten off.

2nd ring: With blue, ch 22, sl ch through first ring (keep right sides of rings up), join with a sl st to form a ring. Ch 1, 40 sc in ring, sl st in beg ch-1. Fasten off.

3rd-7th rings: Make 5 more rings as est, alternating gray and blue and joining through prev ring as est until there are 7 rings, ending with a gray ring.

8th ring: With blue, make another ring as est, joining through first and 7th rings.

9th ring: With green, ch 20. Lay 8-ring square flat with right side up. The 9th ring is the center joining ring and is woven through gray rings as foll: sl green ch under first and 3rd rings, over 3rd and 5th rings, under 5th and 7th

rings, and over 7th and first rings. Join with a sl st in first ch of ch-20 to form a ring. Ch 1, 40 sc in ring, sl st in beg ch-1. Fasten off. Work remainder of square around woven rings.

Rnd 1: Beg with a blue ring in any corner, join blue with a sl st in any sc, ch 4 for first dc and ch 1, sk 1 st, dc in next st, (ch 1, sk 1 st, dc in next st) twice, ch 1, sk 1 st, * (dc, ch 3, dc) in next st for corner, (ch 1, sk 1 st, dc in next st) 4 times = 10 dc in blue corner ring, ch 1, working in next gray ring, dc in any sc, (ch 1, sk 1 st, dc in next st) 4 times = 5 dc in gray ring, ch 1 **, working in next corner ring, dc in any sc, ch 1, sk 1 st, (dc in next st, ch 1, sk 1 st) 3 times, rep from * 3 times more, end last rep at **, sl st in 3rd ch of beg ch-4.

Rnd 2: Ch 1, * sc in ea dc and ch to next corner, work 2 sc in first ch at corner, 3 sc in center ch, sc in 3rd ch of corner sp, rep from * around = 140 sc around, sl st in beg ch-1. Fasten off.

Rnd 3: Join blue with a sl st in any corner, ch 3 for first dc, (dc, ch 3, 2 dc) in same st for corner, * (ch 2, sk 2 sts, dc in ea of next 2 sts) 8 times, ch 2, sk 2 sts, (2 dc, ch 3, 2 dc) in next st for corner, rep from * around, sl st in top of beg ch-3.

Rnd 4: Ch 1, * sc in ea st to next corner, work 3 sc in center ch of corner, 2 sc in next ch of corner, rep from * around = 176 sc around, sl st in beg ch-1. Fasten off.

Rnd 5: Join gray with a sl st in any corner, ch 3 for first dc, (dc, ch 3, 2 dc) in same st for corner, * (ch 1, sk 1 st, dc in next st, ch 1, sk 1 st, work 5 dc in next st, drop last lp from hook, insert hook in first dc of grp, pick up dropped lp and pull through to close popcorn) 10 times, ch 1, sk 1 st, dc in next st, ch 1, sk 1 st, (2 dc, ch 3, 2 dc) in corner, rep from * around, sl st in top of beg ch-3. Fasten off.

Rnd 6: Join green with a sl st in any corner, ch 3 for first dc, (dc, ch 3, 2 dc) in corner sp, * ch 1, sk 1 dc of corner, dc in next dc of corner, (ch 1, popcorn in next dc, ch 1, dc in popcorn) 10 times, ch 1, popcorn in next dc, ch 1, dc in first dc of corner, ch 1, (2 dc, ch 3, 2 dc) in corner sp, rep from * around, sl st in top of beg ch-3. Fasten off.

Rnd 7: Join blue with a sl st in any corner, ch 3 for first dc, (dc, ch 3, 2 dc) in corner sp, * ch 1, sk 1 dc of corner, dc in next dc of corner, (ch 1, popcorn in next dc, ch 1, dc in popcorn) 11 times, ch 1, popcorn in next dc, ch 1, dc in first dc of corner, ch 1, (2 dc, ch 3, 2 dc) in corner sp, rep from * around, sl st in top of beg ch-3. Fasten off.

Rnd 8: Join gray with sc in center ch of any corner, ch 7, sl st in 6th ch from hook, (ch 5, sl st in same st) twice, sc in same st as first sc (corner clover made), * ch 4, sk 2 dc of corner, sc in next dc, [ch 3, sc in next dc bet popcorns, ch 6, sl st in 6th ch from hook, (ch 5, sl st in same st) twice, sc in same dc (clover made), ch 3, sc in next dc] 6 times, ch 4, work corner clover in center ch of corner, rep from * around, sl st in first sc. Fasten off.

Rnd 9: Join green with a sl st in center lp of any corner clover, * ch 12, sc in center lp of next clover, (ch 8, sc in center lp of next clover) 5 times, ch 12, sc in center lp of next corner clover, rep from * around, sl st in base of beg ch-12.

Rnd 10: Ch 3 for first dc, 2 dc in same st, * dc in ea st to next corner, 3 dc in corner, rep from * around, sl st in top of beg ch-3. Fasten off.

Rnd 11: Join blue with a sl st in any corner, ch 3 for first dc, (dc, ch 3, 2 dc) in same st for corner, * ch 1, sk 1 st of corner, dc in next dc, (ch 1, sk 1 st, popcorn in next st, ch 1, sk 1 st, dc in next st) 17 times, ch 1, sk 2 sts, (2 dc, ch 3, 2 dc) in center st of corner, rep from * around, sl st in top of beg ch-3. Fasten off.

Rnd 12: Join gray with a sl st in any corner, ch 3 for first dc, (dc, ch 3, 2 dc) in same sp for corner, * dc in ea st to next corner, (2 dc, ch 3, 2 dc) in corner sp, rep from * around, sl st in top of beg ch-3. Fasten off.

Assembly: Afghan is 3 squares wide and 5 squares long. Be sure all center green rings slant in the same direction. Holding 2 squares with wrong sides facing and working through both pieces, join gray with a sl st in corner, * ch 1, sk 1 st, sl st in bk lp only of next st, rep from * to next corner, cont joining squares as est for a row of 5 squares. Make 2 more rows of 5 squares ea. Join rows as est.

Edging: Rnd 1: With right side facing and afghan turned to work across short edge, join green with a sl st in corner, ch 3 for first dc, (dc, ch 3, 2 dc) in same corner, * (ch 1, sk 1 st, popcorn in next st, ch 1, sk 1 st, dc in next st) 15 times, ch 1, sk 1 st, popcorn in next st, ch 1, dc in joining, rep from * to next corner, omit last dc of last rep, (2 dc, ch 3, 2 dc) in corner sp, cont as est around afghan, sl st in top of beg ch-3.

Rnd 2: Sl st into ch-3 sp, ch 3 for first dc, (dc, ch 3, 2 dc) in same corner, * dc in ea st to next corner, (2 dc, ch 3, 2 dc) in corner sp, rep from * around, sl st in top of beg ch-3. Fasten off.

Rnd 3: Join gray with a sl st in any corner, ch 3 for first dc, (dc, ch 3, 2 dc) in same corner, ch 1, sk 1 st, dc in next st, * (ch 1, sk 1 st, popcorn in next st, ch 1, sk 1 st, dc in next st) to next corner, ch 1, sk 2 dc, (2 dc, ch 3, 2 dc) in corner sp, ch 1, sk 1 st, dc in next st, rep from * around, sl st in top of beg ch-3. Fasten off.

Rnd 4: Join green with a sl st in any corner sp, ch 3 for first dc, (dc, ch 3, 2 dc) in same corner, * dc in ea of next 2 sts, (ch 2, sk across to next popcorn, 2 dc in popcorn) to 3 dc before next corner sp, ch 2, sk 1 dc, dc in ea of next 2 dc, (2 dc, ch 3, 2 dc) in corner sp, rep from * around, sl st in top of beg ch-3. Fasten off.

Rnd 5: Join blue with a sl st in any corner, work 5 sc in same corner, * sc bet next 2 dc, 2 sc bet next 2 dc, (sc bet next 2 dc, 3 sc in next sp) to 4 dc before next corner sp, sc bet next 2 dc, 2 sc bet next 2 dc, sc bet next 2 dc, work 5 sc in corner sp, rep from * around, sl st in first sc. Fasten off.

Rnd 6: Join gray with sc in center st of any corner, * (ch 6, sl st in 5th ch from hook to make a picot) 3 times, ch 1, sk 3 sts, sc in next st (3-picot lp made), ch 9, sl st in 6th ch from hook to make a picot, ch 3, sk 3 sts, sc in next st (single picot lp made), rep from * around working a 3-picot lp before and after ea corner, sl st in first sc. Fasten off.

Rnd 7: Join gray with sc in center picot of next 3-picot lp, (ch 6, sl st in 5th ch from hook to make a picot) 9 times, ch 1, sc in same picot as prev sc (9-picot lp made), * ch 3, sc in picot of next single picot lp, make a 9-picot lp, ch 3, sc in center picot of next lp, make a 9-picot lp, rep from * around working a 9-picot lp in center picot of ea lp, end with ch 3, sl st in first sc. Fasten off.

Pillow square (make 1): With green, ch 8, join with a sl st to form a ring.

Rnd 1: Work 20 sc in ring, sl st in first sc.

Rnd 2: (Ch 10, sl st in same st, sc in ea of next 5 sts) 4 times, sl st in base of beg ch-10.

Rnd 3: Work (15 sc in next ch-10 lp, sc in ea of next 5 sc) 4 times, sl st in first sc, sl st in next sc.

Rnd 4: Ch 4 for first dc and ch 1, sk 1 st, (dc in next st, ch 1, sk 1 st) twice, * 3 dc in next st for corner, (ch 1, sk 1 st, dc in next st) 4 times, (sk 1 st, dc in next st) twice **, (ch 1, sk 1 st, dc in next st) 3 times, ch 1, rep from * around, end last rep at **, ch 1, sl st in 3rd ch of beg ch-4. Fasten off.

Rnd 5: Join gray with a sl st in any center corner st, ch 6 for first dc and ch 3, dc in same st, * ch 1, dc in next st, (ch 1, sk 1 st, dc in next st) 4 times, sk 1 st, dc in next st, ch 1, (sk 1 st, dc in next st, ch 1) 4 times, (dc, ch 3, dc) in next st for corner, rep from * around, sl st in 3rd ch of beg ch-6.

Rnd 6: Ch 5, * sk ch-3 corner sp, sc in next dc, sc in ea of next 6 sts, ch 5, sk 4 dc, sc in next dc, sc in ea of next 6 sts, ch 5, rep from * around, sl st in base of beg ch-5.

Rnd 7: Ch 1, sk 1 ch, * 3 sc in next ch for corner, sk 1 ch, sc in next ch, sc in ea of next 7 sc, sc in ea of next 5 ch, sc in ea of next 7 sc, sc in next ch, sk 1 ch, rep from * around, sl st in beg ch-1. Fasten off.

Rnd 8: Join blue with a sl st in center st of any corner, ch 6 for first dc and ch 3, dc in same st, * (ch 1, sk 1 st, dc in next st) 5 times, (ch 1, dc in next st) 4 times, ch 1, sk 2 sts, dc in next st, (ch 1, sk 1 st, dc in next st) 3 times, ch 1, sk 1 st, (dc, ch 3, dc) in corner, rep from * around, sl st in 3rd ch of beg ch-6.

Rnd 9: Sl st into first ch of corner sp, ch 1, * 3 sc in center ch, sc in ea st to next center corner ch, rep from * around, sl st in first sc of corner, sl st in next sc.

Rnd 10: Ch 3 for first dc, (dc, ch 3, 2 dc) in same st, * (ch 2, sk 2 sts, dc in ea of next 2 sts) 8 times, ch 2, sk 1 st, (2 dc, ch 3, 2 dc) in center corner st, rep from * around, sl st in top of beg ch-3.

Rnds 11-19: Rep rnds 4-12 as for afghan square, changing colors as specified. Fasten off.

Finishing: Use ¼" seam. From polished cotton, cut 16" squares for front and back, and cut 2"-wide bias strips, piecing as needed to measure 1¾ yards. Make 1¾ yards of corded piping. With raw edges aligned, stitch piping to right side of 1 square. Match and slipstitch ends of piping together. With right sides facing, raw edges aligned, and piping toward center, stitch pillow back to front around 3 sides. Turn and insert pillow form. Slipstitch opening closed. Place crocheted square right side up on pillow front and slipstitch to seam.

For Baby

Finished Size
Approximately 51" square.

Materials
Bulky-weight acrylic-polyamide ribbon blend (75-yd. skein): 25 white.

Sizes G and I crochet hooks, or size to obtain gauge.

Gauge
Large square = 30" with size I hook.
Small square = 6" with size I hook.

Directions

Large square (make 1): **Rnd 1:** Wrap yarn around 2 fingers twice, with size I hook pull up a lp through center of ring. Ch 3 for first dc, 11 dc in ring, sl st in top of beg ch-3. Pull beg end of yarn to close center of ring.

Rnd 2: Ch 3 for first dc, dc in same st, * working in bk lps only, dc in ea of next 2 sts, (2 dc, ch 1, 2 dc) in next st for corner, rep from * around, end with 2 dc in same st as beg, ch 1, sl st in top of beg ch-3.

Note: To center corner sts at beg of ea rnd, turn work to wrong side, sl st into ch-1 sp, turn work to right side.

Rnd 3: Ch 3 for first dc, dc in same sp, * working in bk lps only, dc in ea st to next corner sp, (2 dc, ch 1, 2 dc) in next ch-1 sp for corner, rep from * around, end with 2 dc in same sp as beg, ch 1, sl st in top of beg ch-3.

Rnds 4-15: Rep rnd 3 working 4 additional dc bet corners on ea edge = 58 dc bet corner sps after rnd 15.

Rnd 16: Ch 3 for first dc, dc in same sp, * sk next dc, working in bk lps only, dc in ea st to dc before next corner sp, sk dc before corner sp, (2 dc, ch 1, 2 dc) in ch-1 sp for corner, rep from * around, end with 2 dc, ch 1 in same sp as beg, sl st in top of beg ch-3.

Rnds 17-25: Rep rnd 16. Fasten off after rnd 25.

Small square (make 24): With size I hook, ch 4, join with a sl st to form a ring.

Rnd 1: Ch 3 for first dc, 2 dc in ring, (ch 2, 3 dc in ring) 3 times, ch 2, sl st in top of beg ch-3.

Note: Center corner sts at beg of ea rnd as est for large square.

Rnd 2: Ch 4 for first tr, dc in same sp, * hdc in next dc, sc in next dc, hdc in next dc, (dc, tr, ch 2, tr, dc) in next ch-2 sp for corner, rep from * around, end with (dc, tr) in same sp as beg, ch 2, sl st in top of beg ch-4.

Rnd 3: Ch 3 for first dc, dc in same sp, * ch 3, tr in sc, ch 3, (2 dc, ch 2, 2 dc) in corner ch-2 sp, rep from * around, end with 2 dc in same sp as beg, ch 2, sl st in top of beg ch-3.

Rnd 4: Ch 2 for first hdc, hdc in same sp, * hdc in ea of next 2 dc, 3 hdc in next ch-3 sp, hdc in tr, 3 hdc in next ch-3 sp, hdc in ea of next 2 dc, (2 hdc, ch 2, 2 hdc) in corner ch-2 sp, rep from * around, end with 2 hdc in same sp as beg, ch 2, sl st in top of beg ch-2.

Rnd 5: Ch 2 for first hdc, hdc in same sp, * working in bk lps only, hdc in ea st to next corner sp, (2 hdc, ch 2, 2 hdc) in corner ch-2 sp, rep from * around, end with 2 hdc in same sp as beg, ch 2, sl st in top of beg ch-2. Fasten off.

Assembly: Whipstitch 5 small squares together to form a row. Make 3 more rows of 5 small squares each. Whipstitch a row of small squares to each edge of large square. Whipstitch remaining small squares in corners.

Edging: Rnd 1: With size G hook, join yarn with a sl st in any corner, ch 1, sc in same sp, * sc in ea st to next corner, (sc, ch 1, sc) in corner sp, rep from * around, end with sc in beg corner, ch 1, sl st in first sc.

Rnd 2: Sl st in ea of next 11 sts, * sc in next st, (ch 2, sk 1 st, sc in next st) 3 times, ch 10, sk

7 sts, sc in next st, (ch 2, sk 1 st, sc in next st) 3 times, rep from * around, sl st in first sc.

Rnd 3: Ch 1, * sc in next sp, (ch 2, sc in next sp) twice, [(2 dc, ch 2) 5 times, 2 dc] in ch-10 lp, sc in next sp, (ch 2, sc in next sp) twice, sc bet next 2 sts, rep from * around, sl st in first sc.

Rnd 4: Sc in next sp, ch 2, sc in next sp, * (dc in next dc, ch 1, dc in next dc, ch 2) 5 times, dc in next dc, ch 1, dc in next dc, sc in next sp, ch 2, sc in next sp, ch 3 **, sc in next sp, ch 2, sc in next sp, rep from * around, end last rep at **, sl st in first sc.

Rnd 5: Centering first st of rnd as est for large square, sc in same sp, * ch 1, dc in next dc, ch 5, sc in next sp, (ch 4, sc in next sp) 4 times, ch 6, sc in same sp, rep bet ( ) 4 times, ch 5, sk 1 dc, dc in next dc, ch 1, sk 1 sp, sc in next ch-3 sp, rep from * around, sl st in first sc. Fasten off.

Checkerboard

Finished Size

Approximately 54" x 56".

Materials

Sportweight wool-silk blend (115-yd. skein): 19 natural.

Worsted-weight wool (175-yd. skein): 5 blue tweed.

Size G (20"-long) flexible afghan hook, or size to obtain gauge.

Size G crochet hook.

Gauge

5 sts and 4 rows = 1" in afghan st.

Directions

Note: See page 141 for afghan st instructions.

When changing colors, wrap old yarn over new so that no holes occur.

Divide blue yarn into 12 balls. The checkerboard pattern is worked with separate balls of blue and natural yarns as specified in directions.

Bottom border: First checkerboard pat: With natural, ch 230, pull up 10 lps (as specified in row 1, step 1 of afghan st), * join 1 ball of blue and pull up 10 lps, join another skein of natural and pull up 10 lps, rep from * across = 12 natural blocks and 11 blue blocks alternating across.

Work row 1, step 2 of afghan st, using colors as est.

Work 7 rows more afghan st (row 2, steps 1 and 2), using colors as est. Fasten off all yarns.

2nd checkerboard pat: With right side facing and blue, pull up 10 lps, * join natural and pull up 10 lps, join blue and pull up 10 lps, rep from * across.

Work 8 rows afghan st, using colors as est. Fasten off all yarns.

3rd checkerboard pat: With right side facing and natural, pull up 10 lps, * join blue and pull up 10 lps, join natural and pull up 10 lps, rep from * across.

Work 8 rows afghan st, using colors as est. Fasten off all yarns.

Beg body: With right side facing and blue, pull up 10 lps, join natural and pull up 10 lps, join blue and pull up 10 lps, join natural and pull up 170 lps, join blue and pull up 10 lps, join natural and pull up 10 lps, join blue and pull up 10 lps.

Work 8 rows afghan st, using colors as est. Fasten off all yarns used for checkerboard pat.

Work 168 rows afghan st, using natural for center 170 sts and working 3 checkerboard blocks on ea side, alternating colors as est. Fasten off all yarns.

Top border: Rep 2nd checkerboard pat. Fasten off all yarns.

Rep 3rd checkerboard pat. Fasten off all yarns.

Rep 2nd checkerboard pat. Fasten off all yarns.

Border: With natural and size G crochet hook, sc in ea st across top and bottom edges of afghan.

29

Soft Pastel Shells

Finished Size

Throw: Approximately 38" x 48", not including edging.
Robe: Child's size 2.

Materials

Fingering-weight acrylic (170-yd. skein): 6 each green, pink, blue, yellow, lavender for throw; 2 each green, pink, blue, yellow, lavender for robe.

Size F crochet hook, or size to obtain gauge.
32" (½"-wide) lavender satin ribbon.

Gauge

4 dc and 2 rows = 1".

Directions

Throw: *Note:* Work ea row with right side facing.

Row 1: With green, ch 176, sk 1 ch, sc in next ch, [sk 2 ch, 6 dc in next ch (6-dc shell made), sk 2 ch, sc in next ch] 29 times, sc in last ch = 29 shells across. Fasten off. Do not turn.

Row 2: Join pink in first sc of prev row, ch 4 for first tr, 2 tr in same st, * sk 3 dc, sc in center of next shell (bet 3rd and 4th sts of grp), sk next 3 dc and sc, 3 tr in next dc, working in front of 3-tr grp just made, work 3 tr in 5th dc of prev shell (crossover shell made), rep from * across, end with sc in center of next shell, 3 tr in last sc. Fasten off.

Row 3: Join blue in top of beg ch-4 of prev row, ch 1, sc in same st, * sk 2 tr, 6-dc shell in next sc, sc in center of crossover shell, rep from * across, end with sc in last tr. Fasten off.

Row 4: With yellow, rep row 2.

Row 5: With lavender, rep row 3.

Rows 6-90: Rep rows 2 and 3 alternately, working 1 row in ea color and foll est color sequence.

Row 91: With green, rep row 3. Do not fasten off.

Edging: Rnd 1: With throw turned to work across long edge, * sk 2 sts, 5-dc shell in next st, sk 1 st, sc in next st **, rep from * across to corner (work last sc of last rep in corner st), (6-dc shell in same st as row-1 shell, sc in same st as row-1 sc) across to corner (work last sc of last rep in corner st), rep from * to ** across to next corner, ending with sl st in first st of row 91. Fasten off.

Rnd 2: Join pink with sc in center of first shell after corner, * ch 3, (dc, ch 2, dc) in next sc (V-st made), ch 3, sc in center of next shell, rep from * around, end with sl st in first sc. Fasten off. (*Note:* On long edges, work sc in center st of 5-dc shell.)

Rnd 3: Join blue with sc in same st, * ch 12, sk V-st, sc in next sc, (ch 10, sk V-st, sc in next sc) to next corner, rep from * around, end with sl st in first sc. Fasten off.

Rnd 4: Join yellow with sc in same st, rep rnd 3. Fasten off.

Rnd 5: Join lavender with sc in same st, ch 5, working around and over ch-lps on rnds 3 and 4, work a 6-dc shell in ch-2 sp of rnd-2 V-st, * ch 5, sc in next sc, ch 5, 6-dc shell over ch-lps as est, rep from * around, end with sl st in first sc. Fasten off.

Rnd 6: Join green with sl st in center of corner shell, ch 3 for first dc, 2 dc in same sp, * sc in next ch-lp, ch 3, insert hook from front to back under same ch-lp (before rnd-5 sc), bring hook to front of work under next ch-lp (after rnd-5 sc), work 1 sc around these ch-lps (let sc slide up ch-lps), ch 3, sc in ch-lp, work a shell of (3 dc, ch 2, 3 dc) in center of next shell, rep from * around, end with 3 dc, ch 2 in same sp as beg, sl st in top of beg ch. Fasten off.

Rnd 7: Join pink with sl st in ch-2 sp of same shell, ch 3 for first dc, 2 dc in same sp, * ch 3, dc in ea of next 2 ch-sps, ch 3, work a shell of (3 dc, ch 2, 3 dc) in ch-2 sp of next shell, rep from * around, end with 3 dc, ch 2 in same sp as beg, sl st in top of beg ch. Fasten off.

Rnds 8-10: Rep rnd 7, working 1 rnd ea with blue, yellow, and lavender. Fasten off.

Robe back: Rows 1-25: With green, ch 86, work as for throw rows 1-25 = 14 shells across.

Row 26 (shape armhole): With right side facing, sk first shell, join green in next sc, ch 4 for first dc and ch 1, dc in same st, * sc in center of next shell, (dc, ch 1, dc) in next sc (V-st made), rep from * across leaving last shell unworked. Fasten off.

Row 27: Join pink in ch-1 sp of first V-st, ch 3 for first dc, dc in same sp, * dc in next sc, 2 dc in ch-1 sp of next V-st, rep from * across. Fasten off.

Row 28: Join blue in sp bet beg ch-3 and first dc, ch 3 for first dc, sk 1 dc, * dc in next dc, dc in sp bet sts of next 2-dc grp, rep from * across, end with dc in last dc = 26 dc across. Fasten off.

Row 29: Join yellow bet first 2 sts, ch 3 for first dc, dc in same sp, (dc bet next 2 sts, 2-dc grp bet next 2 sts) across. Fasten off.

Row 30: Join lavender bet first 2 sts, ch 3 for first dc, dc in same sp, (sk 1 st, dc in next dc, sk 1 st, 2-dc grp bet next 2 dc) across. Fasten off.

Rows 31-35: Rep row 30, working 1 row ea color and foll est color sequence.

Row 36: With green, rep row 30.

Row 37 (shoulder): Join pink bet first 2 sts, * ch 3 for first dc, dc in same sp, (sk 1 st, dc in next dc, sk 1 st, 2-dc grp bet next 2 dc) 3 times. Fasten off. Sk 18 sts for neck, join pink bet next 2 sts, rep from * across rem sts. Fasten off.

Left front: Rows 1-25: With green, ch 45 and work as for robe back rows 1-25 = 7 shells across.

Row 26 (shape armhole): With right side facing, sk first shell, join green in first sc and rep row 26 of robe back = 7 V-sts across. Fasten off.

Rows 27-33: Work as for robe back rows 27-33.

Row 34 (shape neckline): Join yellow bet first 2 sts, ch 3 for first dc, dc in same sp, (sk 1 st, dc in next dc, sk 1 st, 2-dc grp bet next 2 dc) 3 times. Fasten off.

Rows 35-37: Rep row 34, working 1 row ea with lavender, green, and pink.

Right front: Work as for left front, reversing armhole and neckline shaping.

Assembly: Sew shoulder seams. Sew side seams from bottom edge to underarm.

Edging: Row 1: With right side facing and working across bottom edge of robe, join green with sc in same st as beg of row 1, (6-dc shell in same st as row-1 shell, sc in same st as row-1 sc) across, end with sc in last sc. Fasten off.

Row 2: Join pink with sc in first sc of prev row, ch 5 for first dc and ch 2, dc in same st, (ch 3, sc in center of next shell, ch 3, V-st in next sc) across. Fasten off.

Row 3: Join blue with sc in ch-2 sp of first V-st on prev row, ch 5, sc in next sc, (ch 10, sc in next sc) across to last sc, ch 5, sc in ch-2 sp of last V-st. Fasten off.

Row 4: Join yellow and rep row 3, end with ch 5, sc in last sc. Fasten off.

Row 5: Join lavender with sc in first sc, ch 5, sc in next sc, (ch 5, working around and over ch-lps on rows 3 and 4, work a 6-dc shell in ch-2 sp of row-2 V-st, ch 5, sc in next sc) across. Fasten off.

Row 6: Join green with sc in first sc, ch 3, sc in first ch-sp, * ch 3, sc around ch-lps as est in rnd 6 of throw edging, ch 3, sc in next ch-sp, work a shell of (3 dc, ch 2, 3 dc) in center of next shell, sc in next sp, rep from * across, sc in last sc. Fasten off.

Row 7: Join pink with a sl st in first sc, ch 3 for first dc, 2 dc in same st, ch 3, dc in ea of next 2 ch-sps, * ch 3, work a shell of (3 dc, ch 2, 3 dc) in ch-2 sp of next shell, ch 3, dc in ea of next 2 ch-sps, rep from * across, end with ch 3, 3 dc in last sc. Fasten off.

Rows 8-10: Rep row 7, working 1 row ea with blue, yellow, and lavender. Do not fasten off after row 10.

Note: Work the foll rows up front edge of robe, around neck, and down rem front edge.

Row 1: Work 2 sc in side of ea dc and 1 sc in side of ea sc to corner, (sc, ch 1, sc) in corner st at ea front neck edge, turn.

Row 2: Ch 1, sc in ea st to corner, (sc, ch 1, sc) in corner ch-1 sp at ea front neck edge, turn.

Row 3: Ch 1, sc in ea st to corner ch-1 sp, sc in corner sp, work around neck as foll: ch 3, sk 1 st, * (3 dc, ch 2, 3 dc) in next st, ch 3 **, sc in next st, ch 3, rep from * to next corner ch-1 sp, end last rep at **, sk 1 st, sc in corner sp, sc in ea st across front edge. Fasten off.

Sleeve: Row 1: With right side facing, join green with sc in center of unworked lavender shell on left front at armhole, sk 3 dc, work 6-dc shell in same sc as beg of row 26, work in ends of ea row to shoulder as foll: sk row 26, sc in next row, (sk 1 row, 6-dc shell in next row, sk next row, sc in next row) twice, sk 2 rows, 6-dc shell in shoulder seam, sk 2 rows, sc in next row, rep bet ( ) twice, sk next row, 6-dc shell in next sc (same sc as end of row 26), sc in center of next shell. Fasten off.

Row 2: Join pink with sc in center of beg shell of prev row, work crossover shells (as est in row 2 of throw) across row = 6 shells. Fasten off.

Row 3: Join blue with sc in same st as beg of row 1, 6-dc shell in first sc of row 2, (sc in center of crossover shell, 6-dc shell in next sc) 6 times, end with sc in same st as end of row 1. Fasten off.

Row 4: Join yellow with sc in seam at underarm, sk 1 dc on first row-3 shell, 3 tr in next st, working in front of 3-tr grp just made, work 3 tr in 2nd dc on first row-25 shell (crossover shell made), sc in center of first row-3 shell, cont working crossover shells across row, beg last shell in 5th dc of row-25 shell (before underarm

seam) and end with last shell in 5th dc of last row-3 shell, sl st in first sc of row. Fasten off.

Row 5: Join lavender with sc in center of first crossover shell on prev row, (6-dc shell in next sc, sc in center of next crossover shell) across = 7 shells, sl st in first sc. Fasten off.

Beg working sleeve in rnds. **Rnd 1:** Join green in 2nd dc of first shell on prev row and work crossover shells around, end with sl st in top of beg ch-4 = 7 shells around. Fasten off.

Rnd 2: Join pink with sc in center of crossover shell at underarm, * 6-dc shell in next sc, sc in center of next shell, rep from * around, sl st in first sc = 7 shells around. Fasten off.

Rnds 3-12: Rep rnds 1 and 2 alternately, working 1 rnd ea color and foll est color sequence.

Rnd 13: Join blue in same st as last sl st, ch 4 for first dc and ch 1, dc in same st, * sc in center of next shell, V-st in next sc, rep from * around, sc in center of last shell, sl st in 3rd ch of beg ch-4. Fasten off.

Rnd 14: Join yellow in ch-1 sp of first V-st of prev row, ch 3 for first dc, dc in same sp, dc in next sc, (2 dc in ch-2 sp of next V-st, dc in next sc) around, sl st in top of beg ch-3. Fasten off.

Ruffle: Join lavender with sl st in same st as last sl st, 2 dc in same sp, * ch 3, sk 1 st, sc in next st, ch 3, sk 1 st, (3 dc, ch 2, 3 dc) in next st, rep from * around, end with 3 dc, ch 2 in same sp as beg, sl st in top of beg ch-3. Fasten off.

Rep for other sleeve.

Finishing: Cut ribbon into 2 (16") lengths. Tack 1 ribbon to each side of front, 1" below collar.

Mohair Roses

Finished Size

Approximately 46" x 80".

Materials

Bulky-weight rayon-mohair blend (70-yd. skein): 11 each apricot, eggshell.

Worsted-weight mohair-wool blend (90-yd. skein): 9 variegated pastel.

Size F crochet hook, or size to obtain gauge.

10 yards (1"-wide) ivory wired-edge ribbon.

Gauge

Rose = 6" diameter.
6 dc = 2".

Directions

Block A (make 10): **Rose:** With apricot, ch 6, join with a sl st to form a ring.

Rnd 1: Ch 5 for first dc and ch 2, (dc in ring, ch 2) 7 times, sl st in 3rd ch of beg ch-5.

Rnd 2: Ch 2, 3 dc in next sp, * ch 2, sl st in next dc, ch 2, 3 dc in next sp, rep from * around, end with ch 2, sl st in base of beg ch-2 = 8 petals.

Rnd 3: Holding petals to front of work, * ch 5, sl st from back of work in top of next rnd-1 dc, rep from * around.

Rnd 4: * Ch 2, 4 dc in next lp, ch 2, sl st bet lps, rep from * around.

Rnd 5: * Ch 6, sl st bet next 2 petals as est, rep from * around.

Rnd 6: * Ch 2, 5 dc in next lp, ch 2, sl st bet lps, rep from * around.

Rnd 7: * Ch 7, sl st bet next 2 petals as est, rep from * around.

Rnd 8: * Ch 2, 6 dc in next lp, ch 2, sl st bet lps, rep from * around. Fasten off.

Leaves: Join variegated pastel with a sl st in any sl st bet petals, (ch 8, sl st in 2nd ch from

hook, sc in next ch, hdc in next ch, dc in ea of next 4 ch), sl st in 2nd dc of petal, rep bet ( ), sl st in 5th dc of same petal, rep bet ( ), sl st in next sl st bet petals (3 leaves made). Fasten off. (Sk next petal, join variegated pastel with a sl st in next sl st bet petals, make 3 leaves as est) 3 times. Fasten off.

Border: Rnd 1: Join eggshell with a sl st in tip of any center leaf, * ch 8, sl st in tip of next leaf, ch 15, sl st in center st of next petal, ch 7, sl st in 7th ch of prev ch-15, ch 8, sl st in tip of next leaf, ch 8, sl st in tip of next leaf, rep from * around, end with sl st in same leaf as beg.

Rnd 2: Ch 4 for first tr, 2 tr in same st, * (7 dc in next ch-8 lp) 4 times, 3 tr in sl st of center leaf for corner, rep from * around, end with sl st in top of beg ch-4.

Rnd 3: Sl st into center corner st, ch 4 for first tr, 2 tr in same st, * dc in next tr, dc in ea of next 6 dc, keeping last lp of ea st on hook, dc in ea of next 2 dc, yo and pull through all lps on hook (dec over 2 sts made), (dc in ea of next 5 dc, dec over next 2 dc) twice, dc in ea of next 6 dc, dc in first tr of corner, 3 tr in center corner st, rep from * around, end with sl st in top of beg ch-4.

Rnd 4: Sl st into center corner st, ch 5 for first tr and ch 1, (tr, ch 1, tr) in same st, * dc in ea st to next corner, (tr, ch 1, tr, ch 1, tr) in center corner st, rep from * around, end with sl st in 4th ch of beg ch-5.

Rnd 5: Sl st into center corner st, ch 3 for first dc, 2 dc in same st, * dc in ch-1 sp, dc in ea st to next corner, dc in ch-1 sp, 3 dc in center corner st, rep from * around, end with sl st in top of beg ch-3.

Rnd 6: Sl st into center corner st, ch 3 for first dc, 2 dc in same st, * dc in ea st to next corner, 3 dc in center corner st, rep from * around, end with sl st in top of beg ch-3. Fasten off.

Block B (make 5): Rep directions for block A working colors as foll: use apricot for rose, use eggshell for leaves, use variegated pastel for border.

Assembly: Arrange blocks in 3 rows of 5 squares ea with a block B in ea corner and in center of middle row.

First block: Join apricot in corner of block B, * ch 4 for first tr, tr in same st, sk 4 sts, tr in next st, ch 4, sl st in same st, (ch 4, tr in same st, sk 3 sts, tr in next st, ch 4, sl st in same st) 7 times, ch 4, tr in same st, sk 4 sts, tr in next st, ch 4, sl st in same st for corner, rep from * around for 9 lps on ea edge of block. Fasten off.

2nd block: Join apricot in corner of block A, ch 4, tr in same st, sl st in center of corresponding lp on first block, sk 4 sts on 2nd block, tr in next st, ch 4, sl st in same st, (ch 4, tr in same st, sl st in center of corresponding lp on first block, sk 3 sts on 2nd block, tr in next st, ch 4, sl st in same st) to corner, cont around block as est for first block.

Join rem blocks as est. At ea intersection of 4 blocks, work a grp of 4-tr petals as foll: in last corner of 4th block in a grp, ch 4 in same corner as last sl st, keeping last lp of ea st on hook, work 1 tr in same corner, work 2 tr in corner st of ea of 3 adjacent blocks, yo and pull through all lps on hook (4-tr petals made). Fasten off.

Finishing: Cut 4 (48") lengths and 2 (82") lengths of ribbon. Weave ribbons through joining stitches, being careful to keep ribbons flat. Fold 1" at each end of ribbon to back and tack to secure.

Black and White

Black and White

Finished Size

Approximately 50" x 70".

Materials

Worsted-weight wool-acrylic blend (103-yd. ball): 17 white/black tweed (A).

Worsted-weight acrylic (110-yd. ball): 16 black (B).

Fingering-weight acrylic-wool-mohair blend (240-yd. ball): 2 white (C).

Worsted-weight acrylic-nylon blend (130-yd. ball): 3 black (D).

Size E crochet hook, or size to obtain gauge.

Gauge

4 dc and 2 rows = 1".
Square = 10".

Directions

Square 1 (make 17): With A, ch 6, join with a sl st to form a ring.

Rnd 1: Work 16 sc in ring, sl st in first sc.

Rnd 2: Ch 3 for first dc, working in bk lps only, dc in ea of 2 sc, * (dc, ch 1, dc) in next sc for corner, dc in ea of 3 sc, rep from * around, sl st in top of beg ch-3, turn.

Rnd 3: Ch 3 for first dc, working in ft lps only, dc in next dc, * 3 dc in ch-1 sp for corner, dc in ea of 2 dc, (yo and insert hook in st, yo and pull up a lp) 5 times in next dc, yo and pull through all lps on hook, ch 1 (puff made), dc in ea of 2 dc, rep from * around, end with sl st in top of beg ch-3, turn.

Rnd 4: Ch 3 for first dc, working in bk lps only, * dc in ea dc, puff, and ch-1 to next corner, 3 dc in center corner st, rep from * around, sl st in top of beg ch-3, turn.

Rnd 5: Ch 3 for first dc, working in ft lps only, puff in next st, dc in ea of 2 dc, (3 dc in next st for corner, dc in ea of 2 sts, puff in next st, dc in ea of 4 sts, puff in next st, dc in ea of next 2 sts) 3 times, 3 dc in next st, dc in ea of 2 sts, puff in next st, dc in ea of 3 sts, sl st in top of beg ch-3, turn.

Rnd 6: Ch 3 for first dc, working in bk lps only, * dc in ea dc, puff, and ch-1 to next corner, 5 dc in center corner st, rep from * around, end with sl st in top of beg ch-3 = 76 sts around. Fasten off. Do not turn.

Rnd 7: Working in bk lps only, join B with a sl st in center dc of any corner, ch 2 for first hdc, 2 hdc in same st, * hdc in ea of 4 sts, yo and insert hook around post of dc 2 rows below (st before first row-5 puff), yo and pull up a lp, complete st as a dc (long dc made), sk st behind long dc just made, hdc in ea of 8 sts, long dc around post of dc 2 rows below (st after 2nd row-5 puff), sk st behind long dc just made, hdc in ea of 4 sts, 3 hdc in next st for corner, rep from * around, end with sl st in top of beg ch-2, turn.

Rnd 8: Ch 2 for first hdc, working in ft lps only, hdc in ea of 2 sts, * puff in next st, hdc in ea of 5 sts, puff in next st, hdc in ea of 6 sts, puff in next st, hdc in ea of 3 sts, 3 hdc in next st for corner, hdc in ea of 3 sts, rep from * around, end with sl st in top of beg ch-2, turn.

Rnd 9: Ch 2 for first hdc, working in bk lps only, hdc in next st, * 5 hdc in next st for corner, hdc in ea hdc, puff, and ch-1 to center st of next corner, rep from * around, end with sl st in top of beg ch-2 = 120 sts around. Fasten off. Do not turn.

Rnd 10: Working in bk lps only, join C with sl st in center hdc of any corner, ch 2 for first hdc, 2 hdc in same st, * hdc in ea of next 4 sts, long dc around post of hdc 2 rows below (2 sts before first row-8 puff), sk st behind long dc just made, hdc in ea of next 6 sts, long dc around post of hdc 2 rows below (2 sts before next puff), sk st behind long dc just made, hdc in ea of next 5 hdc, long dc around post of hdc 2 rows below (2 sts after same puff), sk st behind long dc just made, hdc in ea of next 6 hdc, long dc around post of hdc 2 rows below (2 sts after next puff), sk st behind long dc just made, hdc in ea of next 4 hdc, 3 hdc in next st for corner, rep from * around, end with sl st in top of beg ch-2. Fasten off. Do not turn.

Rnd 11: Working in bk lps only, join D with sl st in center hdc of any corner, ch 2 for first hdc, 4 hdc in same st, * hdc in ea st to next corner, 5 hdc in center corner st, rep from * around, end with sl st in beg ch-2. Fasten off. Do not turn.

Rnd 12: Working in bk lps only, join A with sl st in center hdc of any corner, ch 2 for first hdc, 2 hdc in same st, * hdc in ea st to next corner, 3 hdc in center corner st, rep from * around, end with sl st in top of beg ch-2, turn.

Rnd 13: Ch 2 for first hdc, working in ft lps only, hdc in ea of next 11 sts, * puff in next st, hdc in ea of next 11 sts, puff in next st, hdc in ea of next 12 sts, 3 hdc in next st for corner, hdc in ea of next 12 sts, rep from * 3 times more, 3 hdc in next st for corner, sl st in top of beg ch-2, turn.

Rnd 14: Ch 2 for first hdc, working in bk lps only, hdc in next st, (3 hdc in next st for corner, hdc in ea of 41 sts) 3 times, 3 hdc in next st for corner, hdc in ea of 39 sts, sl st in beg ch-2. Fasten off.

Square 2 (make 18): Rep square 1, working colors in foll sequence: B, A, D, C, B.

Assembly: Afghan is 5 squares wide and 7 squares long. Beg with square 2 (dark center) in corner, arrange squares in checkerboard pat, alternating light and dark centers.

Holding 2 squares with wrong sides facing and working through both pieces, join B with sl st in center corner st, * ch 1, sk 1 st, sl st in next st, rep from * to next corner st, pick up next 2 squares and cont as est, beg in center corner st and working to next center corner st. Fasten off after 7 pairs of squares have been joined.

(Join 7 squares to assembled squares as est) 3 times for 5 rows with 7 squares ea. Join rows as est, working a sl st over the joining bet squares. Fasten off after ea row.

Edging: *Note:* Work edging with same yarn as center of ea square. Hdc in joining is always worked with B. To change yarns, yo and pull through new color to complete last st of old color. Join B with a sl st in any corner, ch 1, 2 sc in same st, * sc in ea st across square to within 2 sts of joining, hdc in ea of next 2 sts, hdc in joining, change to A and fasten off B. Cont with A across next square, hdc in ea of next 2 sts, sc in ea st to within 2 sts of next joining, hdc in ea of next 2 sts, change to B and fasten off A. With B, hdc in joining, hdc in ea of next 2 sts, rep from * to corner of afghan, work 3 sc in corner, rep from * around, changing colors as est to match center of ea square.

Artist's Palette

Finished Size

Approximately 62" x 96".

Materials

Fingering-weight cotton-blend bouclé (170-yd. ball): 34 variegated pink/yellow/blue/green.

Size E crochet hook, or size to obtain gauge.

Gauge

Square = 9".

Directions

Note: To make a qdtr, yo 5 times. To make a quin tr, yo 6 times.

Square (make 54): Ch 16, join with a sl st to form a ring.

Rnd 1: Ch 1, 24 sc in ring, sl st in first sc = 24 sts.

Rnd 2: Ch 1, sc in same st, * ch 4, keeping last lp of ea st on hook, dtr in ea of next 2 sts, yo and pull through all lps on hook (2-dtr cl made), work a grp of 3 leaves in 2-dtr cl as foll: (ch 8, qdtr, ch 7, sc, ch 8, quin tr, ch 8, sc, ch 7, qdtr, ch 7, sl st), ch 4, sc in next st of rnd 1, ch 7, sk 2 sts, sc in next st, rep from * 3 times more, sl st in first sc. Fasten off.

Rnd 3: Join yarn with a sl st in sp before quin tr of next center leaf, ch 1, sc in same sp, * ch 2, sk quin tr, sc in next ch, ch 5, sc just before and after next qdtr of next leaf, ch 7, sc just before and after qdtr of first leaf of next grp, ch 5, sc just before quin tr of next leaf, rep from * around, sl st in first sc.

Rnd 4: Ch 1, sc in same st, * 3 sc in next ch-2 sp for corner, sc in next sc, sc in ea of next 5 ch, sc in ea of next 2 sc, sc in ea of next 7 ch, sc in ea of next 2 sc, sc in ea of next 5 ch, sc in next sc, rep from * around, sl st in first sc.

Rnd 5: Sl st into center st of corner, ch 3 for first dc, 2 dc in same st, * dc in ea st to next corner, 3 dc in center corner st, rep from * around, sl st in top of beg ch-3.

Rnd 6: Ch 3 for first dc, 2 dc in same st, work a crossed st over next 2 sts as foll: * (sk 1 st, dc in next st, working behind dc just made, dc in sk st) 14 times, 3 dc in center corner st, rep from * around, sl st in top of beg ch-3.

Rnd 7: Sl st into center corner st, ch 1, 3 sc in same st, * sc in ea st to next corner, 3 sc in center corner st, rep from * around, sl st in first sc.

Rnd 8: Sl st into center corner st, ch 4 for first tr, (2-tr cl, ch 2, 3-tr cl) in same st for corner, * ch 5, sk 3 sts, 3-tr cl in next st, (ch 5, sk 4 sts, 3-tr cl in next st) 5 times, ch 5, sk 3 sts, (3-tr cl, ch 2, 3-tr cl) in center corner st, rep from * around, sl st in top of beg ch-4.

Rnd 9: Sl st into corner ch-2 sp, ch 5, sc in 4th ch from hook to make a picot, sc in same sp, ch-4 picot, sc in same sp, * (ch-4 picot, sc in next ch-5 sp, ch-4 picot, sc in next cl) 6 times, ch-4 picot, sc in next sp, ch-4 picot, sc in corner ch-2 sp, (ch-4 picot, sc) twice in same corner, rep from * around, sl st in first sc. Fasten off.

Assembly: Afghan is 6 squares wide and 9 squares long. Lay 2 squares side by side with right sides up. Join yarn with sc in corner picot of left-hand square. (*Note:* There are 2 picots in ea corner sp, be sure to use the 1 on the side being worked.)

Ch 2, hdc in corresponding picot on 2nd square, turn work ¼ turn to the right, ch 2, work 3 hdc around beg ch-2, * hdc in next picot on first square, ch 2, sl st in top of ch-2 made after the turn, hdc in next picot on 2nd square, ch 2, ¼ turn, hdc around hdc just made, sk ch-2, 2 hdc around hdc which joined prev picot on first square, ¼ turn, rep from * across edge to join all picots, including 1 picot at ea corner.

Cont joining squares as est for a row of 9 squares. Make 5 more rows with 9 squares ea. Lay 2 rows side by side with right sides up and join as est. To join seams, work sts as est for picots. Fasten off.

Hearth & Home

*The new decor is finally
finished, and you
are ready to add those
personal touches that make your
home distinctive. To express
your individual style, choose
from an eye-catching array of
decorative items, like an
elegant mantel swag
or a throw pillow covered
with flowers.*

Shades of Violet

Pictured on preceding pages.

Finished Size

Approximately 16" square.

Materials

Fingering-weight mercerized cotton (184-yd. ball): 9 mauve, 2 light green, 9 purple.

Size #1 steel crochet hook, or size to obtain gauge.

1¼ yards (45"-wide) purple polished cotton fabric.

Sewing thread to match fabric.

2 yards (½") cording.

16"-square pillow form.

Gauge

Square = 9".

Directions

Flower (make 4): **Rnd 1:** With mauve, ch 6, sl st in 6th ch from hook, (ch 5, sl st in same ch) 5 times = 6 lps.

Rnd 2: Ch 1, (sc, hdc, 3 dc, hdc, sc) in ea lp around, sl st in beg ch-1.

Rnd 3: Holding petals to front of work, * ch 6, sc from back of work bet next 2 petals, rep from * around, sl st in base of beg ch.

Rnd 4: Ch 1, (sc, hdc, 5 dc, hdc, sc) in ea lp around, sl st in beg ch-1.

Rnd 5: * Ch 8, sc bet next 2 petals as est, rep from * around, sl st in base of beg ch.

Rnd 6: Ch 1, (sc, hdc, 9 dc, hdc, sc) in ea lp around, sl st in beg ch-1. Fasten off.

Leaves: Join green with a sl st in first dc of 9-dc grp on any petal, (ch 7, sc in 2nd ch from hook, sc in next ch, hdc in ea of next 2 ch, dc in next ch, hdc in next ch, sc in same st as sl st), ch 10, sc in 2nd ch from hook, sc in next ch, hdc in ea of next 2 ch, dc in ea of next 3 ch, hdc in ea of next 2 ch, sc in same st as beg, rep bet ( ) once more (3 leaves made). Fasten off. Sk across to last dc of 9-dc grp on next petal, make 3 leaves as est, sk next petal, work 3 leaves in first dc of 9-dc grp on next petal, work 3 leaves in last dc of 9-dc grp on next petal (4 grps of 3 leaves ea).

First square border: Rnd 1: Join purple with a sl st in tip of any center leaf, ch 1, 2 sc in same st, * ch 8, sc in tip of next leaf, ch 9, sc in tip of first leaf of next grp, ch 8, 3 sc in tip of center leaf, rep from * around, end with sc in same st as beg, sl st in first sc.

Note: Work in bk lps only for rnds 2-7.

Rnd 2: Ch 1, 2 sc in same st, * sc in ea st to next corner, 3 sc in corner st, rep from * around, end with sc in same st as beg, sl st in first sc = 31 sts bet corners.

Rnd 3: Ch 1, 2 sc in same st, (sc in ea of next 3 sts, 5 dc in next st, drop last lp from hook, insert hook in first dc of grp, pick up dropped lp, draw through and tighten to close popcorn) 7 times, sc in ea of next 3 sts, 3 sc in corner, rep from * around, end with sc in beg corner, sl st in first sc = 7 popcorns on ea side of square.

Rnd 4: Ch 1, 2 sc in same st, * sc in ea sc and popcorn to next corner, 3 sc in corner, rep from * around, end with sc in beg corner, sl st in first sc.

Rnd 5: Ch 3 for first dc, dc in same st, * dc in ea st to next corner, 5 dc in corner, rep from * around, end with 3 dc in beg corner, sl st in top of beg ch-3.

Rnd 6: Ch 1, 2 sc in same st, * sc in ea of next 5 sts, (popcorn in next st, sc in ea of next 3 sts) 8 times, sc in ea of next 2 sts, 3 sc in corner, rep from * around, end with sc in beg corner, sl st in first sc.

Rnd 7: Ch 1, 2 sc in same st, * sc in ea sc and popcorn to next corner, 3 sc in corner, rep from * around, end with sc in beg corner, sl st in first sc. Fasten off.

Rnd 8: Join mauve with a sl st in any corner,

ch 4 for first dc and ch 1, dc in same st, * (ch 1, sk 1 st, dc in next st) to next corner, ch 1, (dc, ch 1) twice in corner, dc in same corner, rep from * around, end with (dc, ch 1) in beg corner, sl st in 3rd ch of beg ch-4. Fasten off.

Rnd 9: Join purple with a sl st in center ch-1 sp of any corner, ch 3 for first dc of popcorn, complete popcorn as est, popcorn in next ch-1 sp, sc in next dc, * [ch 5, sc in 2nd ch from hook, hdc in next ch, dc in ea of next 2 ch, sk 1 dc on square, sc in next dc (wedge made)] to next corner, popcorn in ea ch-1 sp of corner, sc in next dc, rep from * around, end with popcorn in ch-1 sp of beg corner, sl st in top of beg ch-3. Fasten off.

2nd square border: Work as for first square border rnds 1-8.

Rnd 9 (joining rnd): Work as for rnd 9 of first square border through 3rd corner, sc in last dc of corner, * ch 5, sl st in tip of corresponding wedge on first square, complete wedge on 2nd square

as est, sk 1 dc on 2nd square, sc in next dc, rep from * across, finish last corner of 2nd square as est for first square. Fasten off.

Make and join 2 more squares to complete pillow top (see photo).

Finishing: Use ½" seam. From polished cotton, cut 17" squares for front and back, and cut 3"-wide bias strips, piecing as needed to measure 2 yards. Make 2 yards of covered cording. With raw edges aligned, stitch piping to right side of 1 square. Match and slipstitch ends of piping together. With right sides facing, raw edges aligned, and piping toward center, stitch pillow back to front around 3 sides. Turn and insert pillow form. Slipstitch opening closed. Place crocheted piece right side up on pillow front, align top edge of mauve stitches (round 8) with edge of pillow and slipstitch to seam. Tack center popcorns to pillow front (see photo).

Bolster Pillow

Materials

Size 10 crochet cotton (400-yd. ball): 4 aqua.

Size #10 steel crochet hook, or size to obtain gauge.

65" x 36" piece of flowered chintz fabric to match crochet.

Sewing thread to match crochet and fabric.

2 (40" x 45") pieces of batting.

7⅔ yards (¼"-wide) satin ribbon to match crochet.

10¼ yards (⅛"-wide) satin ribbon to match crochet.

Gauge

12 sc and 10 rows = 1".

Directions

Note: The foll directions will make 1 (6" x 33") piece of edging. Rep all crochet directions 3 times more for 4 pieces.

Scallops: Ch 30.

Row 1: Sc in 2nd ch from hook and ea ch across = 29 sc, ch 1, turn.

Note: Work all sc sts through ft lps only, unless otherwise specified.

Row 2: Sc in ea of next 27 sc, sk rem 2 sc, ch 1, turn.

Rows 3, 5, and 7: Sc in ea sc across, ch 1, turn.

Row 4: Sc in ea of next 22 sc, sk rem 5 sc, ch 1, turn.

Row 6: Sc in ea of next 17 sc, sk rem 5 sc, ch 1, turn.

Row 8: Sc in ea of next 10 sc, sk rem 7 sc, ch 1, turn.

Row 9: Sc in ea sc across, do not turn, ch 16.

Row 10: Sc in 2nd ch from hook and ea of next 9 ch = 10 sc, sk rem 5 ch for sp bet scallops, ch 1, turn.

Row 11: Sc in ea sc across = 10 sc, ch 8, turn. *Note:* Be sure to keep inc ch straight. After turn, with wrong side of ch facing, work in top lps only.

Row 12: Sc in 2nd ch from hook and ea rem ch, sc in ea sc = 17 sc, ch 1, turn.

Row 13: Sc in ea sc across, ch 6, turn.

Row 14: Sc in 2nd ch from hook and ea rem ch, sc in ea sc = 22 sc.

Row 15: Sc in ea sc across, ch 6, turn.

Row 16: Sc in 2nd ch from hook and ea rem ch, sc in ea sc = 27 sc.

Row 17: Sc in ea sc across, ch 3, turn.

Row 18: Sc in 2nd ch from hook and ea rem ch, sc in ea sc = 29 sc.

Rep rows 2-18, 13 times more for 13 scallops with a half-scallop at ea end. Fasten off after last rep.

Edging: With right side facing and scallops pointing up, join thread with a sl st in point of first half-scallop. * Ch 5 for first dc and ch 2, dc in same st, ch 2, dc in first sc of next ridge, (ch 2, sk 1 sc, dc in next sc, ch 2, dc in first sc of next ridge) twice, (ch 3, sk 2 sc, dc in next sc) twice, ch 3, dc in first sc of next ridge, (ch 2, sk 2 sc, dc in next sc) twice, ch 3, sk last sc, sl st in 3rd ch of ch-5 sp bet scallops, working down side of 2nd scallop, ch 3, sl st in top of dc just made, sk first sc of next scallop, dc in next sc, ch 2, sl st in top of next dc of prev scallop, sk 2 sc of 2nd scallop, dc in next sc, ch 2, sl st in top of next dc of prev scallop, sk 2 sc of 2nd scallop, dc in next sc (at point of ridge), ch 3, sk 3 sc, dc in next sc, ch 3, dc in last sc of ridge, (ch 2, sk 1 sc, dc in next sc, ch 2, dc in last sc of ridge) twice, ch 2, dc in point of scallop, rep from * to end of piece, end with ch 2, dc in same point of last half-scallop. Fasten off.

Header: With right side facing and straight edge of scallops at top, join thread with a sl st in corner st of first half-scallop.

Row 1: Ch 6 for first tr and ch 2, sk 1 row, tr in next row, (ch 2, sk 1 row, tr in next row) 3 times, * ch 2, sk ch-sp, tr in sl st, ch 2, sk ch-sp, tr in corner of next scallop **, (ch 2, sk 1 row, tr in next row) 8 times, rep from * across, end last rep at **, (ch 2, sk 1 row, tr in next row) 3 times, ch 2, tr in corner, ch 4, turn.

Row 2: * (Tr, ch 4, sl st, ch 4, tr) in next tr, ch 1, sk next tr, rep from * across, end with tr in top of last tr of prev row, turn.

Row 3: Ch 6 for first tr and ch 2, keeping last lp of ea st on hook, work 2 tr in last tr of prev row, yo and pull through all lps on hook (2-tr cl made), ch 1, * (tr, ch 4, sl st, ch 4, tr) in next ch-1 sp, ch 1, rep from * across, end with 2-tr cl in top of tch, ch 2, tr in same st, turn.

Row 4: Sl st in same tr, ch 2, sl st in next sp, * ch 5, sl st in next sp, rep from * across, end with ch 2, sl st in 4th ch of tch. Fasten off.

Flower insert: Ch 12, join with a sl st to form a ring. Keeping last lp of ea st on hook, ch 4 for first tr, 3 tr in same st, yo and through all lps on hook (cl made), (ch 9, sk 1 ch of ring, 4-tr cl in next ch) 3 times = 4 petals.

Note: Be sure to keep ch straight and right side facing. Always sl st from right side of work.

With right sides up, position scallop piece with header at top and hold flower with unworked portion of ring aligned with the sp bet a pair of scallops, cont working flower as foll: Ch 4, sl st in 2nd dc of edging (not counting sts at point of scallop), ch 4, sk 1 ch of ring, 4-tr cl in next ch of ring, ch 9, sk 3 dc on edging, sl st in next dc, ch 4, sl st in corresponding dc of next scallop, ch 4, sl st in center ch of prev ch-9, ch 4, sk 1 ch of ring, 4-tr cl in next ch of ring, ch 4, sk 3 dc on edging (2nd scallop), sl st in next dc (corresponds to sts on first scallop), ch 4, sl st in top of first cl. Fasten off.

Rep flower insert directions 13 times more for a flower bet ea pair of scallops.

Ruffle: With right side facing and flowers at top, join thread with a sl st in 3rd ch of ch-5 at point of first half-scallop, ch 3 for first dc.

Row 1: * Ch 4, dc in 5th ch of ch-9, (ch 13, dc in 5th ch of next ch-9) twice, ch 4, dc in ch-5 at point of next scallop, rep from * across, end with dc in last dc at point of last half-scallop, ch 4, turn.

Row 2: * Tr in next dc, (ch 2, sk 1 ch, tr in next ch) 6 times, ch 2, sk 1 ch, tr in next dc **, (ch 2, sk 1 ch, tr in next ch) 6 times, ch 2, tr in ch before next dc, tr in first ch of next ch-4 sp, ch 2, sk next dc, tr in last ch of next ch-4 sp, rep from * across, end last rep at **, sk 4 ch, tr in next ch (3rd ch of tch above point of scallop), ch 3, turn.

Row 3: Sk first tr and ch-2 sp, * dc in next tr, (2 dc in next ch-2 sp, dc in next tr) 13 times, sk across next 3 ch-2 sps, rep from * across, end with dc in tch, ch 4, turn.

Row 4: Sk 3 dc, tr in next dc, * (ch 4, sk 2 dc, tr in next dc) 11 times, sk last 3 dc, rep from * across, end with tr in tch, ch 3, turn.

Row 5: * Sk first tr, 3 dc in next sp, (dc in next tr, 3 dc in next sp) 10 times, sk last tr, rep from * across, end with dc in tch, ch 3, turn.

Row 6: * Sk first dc, dc in next dc, (ch 5, sl st in 5th ch from hook to make a picot, ch 1, sk 1 dc, dc in next dc) 20 times, sk last dc, rep from * across, end with dc in tch. Fasten off.

Edging for sides and header: With right side facing and piece turned to work across beg half-scallop edge, join thread with a sl st in top of beg ch-3 of row 6 on ruffle, ch 7 for first tr and ch 3, (tr in top of next dc, ch 3, tr in top of next ch-4, ch 3) twice, (tr in top of next dc, ch 3) twice, tr in first sc of scallop, (ch 3, sk 3 sc, tr in next sc) 7 times, ch 3, tr in top of next ch-4, ch 3, tr in top of next tr, ch 3, (tr, ch 7, tr) in top of next ch-4 for corner, ch 2, sk ch-2, tr in next sl st, * ch 2, tr in center of ch-5, ch 2, tr in next sl st, rep from * across to next corner, ch 2, sk ch-2, (tr, ch 7, tr) in next tr for corner, ch 3, tr in top of next tr, ch 3, tr in top of next ch-4, ch 3, tr in first sc of scallop, (ch 3, sk 3 sc, tr in next sc) 7 times, (ch 3, tr in top of next dc, ch 3, tr in top of next ch-4) twice, ch 3, tr in top of next tr, ch 3, tr in top of next dc, ch 3, tr in top of last dc. Fasten off.

Assembly: Match and whipstitch ends of 1 piece together. Repeat for other 3 pieces.

With right sides up and pattern aligned, layer 2 pieces so that bottom edge of first overlaps top edge of 2nd about 2" (see photo). Slipstitch top edge of bottom piece to wrong side of 2nd piece. Repeat for 2 remaining pieces.

Finishing: Use ¼" seam. Finish 36" edges of chintz with a ¼" hem. With right sides facing, stitch 65" edges together to form a tube. Turn. Slipstitch 1 crocheted edging around each end of tube. Layer batting pieces and roll tightly to form a 45"-long round pillow form. Insert form in fabric tube. Cut ribbons into 46" lengths. Tie 7 ribbon lengths around fabric at each end of pillow form.

Have a Seat

Have a Seat

Finished Size

Heart: Approximately 13" x 13".
Round: Approximately 14" diameter.

Materials (for 1 set)

Sportweight viscose-acrylic-lurex blend (76-yd. ball): 5 black with multicolor slubs.
Size G crochet hook, or size to obtain gauge.

Gauge

4 dc = 1".
1 row sc and 1 row dc = 1".

Directions

Heart chair back: Ch 11, 2 tr and 1 dc in 5th ch from hook.

Rnd 1: Work 2 dc in next ch, dc in next ch, hdc in ea of next 3 ch, sc in next ch, ch 3, sl st in first ch of beg ch-11 to make a picot (point of heart), working across opposite side of beg ch-11, sc in same ch, hdc in ea of next 3 ch, dc in next ch, 2 dc in next ch, dc and 2 tr in next ch, ch 3, sl st in same ch as beg.

Rnd 2: Sl st in ea of next 3 ch, hdc in next ch, 3 dc in next tr, 2 tr in ea of next 2 sts, 2 dc in next st, dc in ea of next 3 sts, hdc in ea of next 3 sts, (sc, ch-3 picot, sc) in picot, hdc in ea of next 3 sts, dc in ea of next 3 sts, 2 dc in next st, 2 tr in ea of next 2 sts, 3 dc in next st, hdc in top of ch-3, sl st in ea ch to center of heart.

Rnd 3: Sl st in ea of next 3 sl sts, hdc and dc in next st, 2 dc in next st, 2 tr in ea of next 3 sts, 2 dc in next st, dc in ea of next 8 sts, hdc in ea of next 2 sts, (sc, ch-3 picot, sc) in picot, hdc in ea of next 2 sts, dc in ea of next 8 sts, 2 dc in next st, 2 tr in ea of next 3 sts, 2 dc in next st, dc and hdc in next st, sl st in next st, turn.

Note: Work in rows for remainder of piece.

Row 1: Ch 1, sk next sl st and hdc, sc in next st, * (yo and pull up a lp) 5 times in next st, yo and through all lps on hook (puff made), ch 2, sk 1 st, rep from * 9 times more, puff in picot at point of heart, ch 2, sk 2 sts, puff in next st, (ch 2, sk 1 st, puff in next st) 9 times, ch 1, sc in next st, sk 1 st, sl st in next st, turn = 21 puffs.

Row 2: Sk sl st, sc in next st, sc in ea puff and ch to point of heart = 31 sc, (sc, ch-3 picot, sc) in puff at point of heart, sc in ea ch and puff to top of heart = 30 sc, sc in next ch, sl st in next st, turn.

Row 3: Sk sl st, sc in ea of next 2 sts, hdc in next st, dc in ea of next 29 sts to picot, (dc, ch-3 picot, dc) in picot, dc in ea of next 29 sts, hdc in next st, sc in ea of next 2 sts, turn.

Row 4: Sk 1 st, sc in ea of next 32 sts, (sc, ch-3 picot, sc) in picot, sc in ea of next 32 sts, sl st in next st, turn.

Row 5: Sk sl st, sc in ea of next 2 sts, (hdc, ch 2, dc) in next st, (ch 2, sk 1 st, dc in next st) 15 times, ch 2, (dc, ch-3 picot, dc) in picot, ch 2, dc in next st, (ch 2, sk 1 st, dc in next st) 14 times, ch 2, (dc, ch 2, hdc) in next st, sc in ea of next 2 sts, sl st in next st, turn.

Row 6: Sk sl st, sc in ea of next 5 sts, hdc in ea of next 19 sts, sc in ea of next 30 sts to picot, (sc, ch-3 picot, sc) in picot, sc in ea of next 30 sts, hdc in ea of next 19 sts, sc in ea of next 5 sts, turn.

Row 7: Sk first st, sc in ea of next 2 sts, hdc in next st, (puff in next st, ch 2, sk 1 st) 3 times, puff in next st, (ch 2, sk 2 sts, puff in next st) 14 times, ch 2, sk 1 st, puff in next st, ch 2, puff in picot, ch-3 picot, ch 2, puff in next st, ch 2, sk 1 st, puff in next st, (ch 2, sk 2 sts, puff in next st) 14 times, (ch 2, sk 1 st, puff in next st) 3 times, ch 1, hdc in next st, sc in ea of next 2 sts, sl st in next st, turn.

Row 8: Sk sl st, sc in ea ch and puff to point of heart = 60 sc, (sc, ch-3 picot, sc) in picot, sc in ea ch and puff to top of heart = 58 sc, sc in ea of next 2 sts, turn.

Row 9: Sk first st, sc in ea of next 2 sts, hdc in ea of next 20 sts, (sk 1 st, dc in next st) 18 times, (dc, ch-3 picot, dc) in picot, dc in next st, (sk 1 st, dc in next st) 18 times, dc in ea of next 20 sts, hdc in next st, sc in ea of next 2 sts, turn.

Row 10: Ch 1, sk first st, sc in ea st to picot = 42 sc, (sc, ch-3 picot, sc) in picot, sc in ea of next 42 sts, 16 sc down to center of heart, sl st in center st, 16 sc up rem side of heart, sl st in next sc. Fasten off.

Tie (make 2): Ch 94, hdc in 3rd ch from hook and ea ch across. Fasten off.

To attach crochet to chair, thread ties through last round (see photo).

Round seat cover: Ch 4, join with a sl st to form a ring.

Rnd 1 (right side): Work 8 sc in ring.

Rnd 2: Working in ft lps only, 2 sc in ea st around = 16 sts.

Rnd 3: Ch 3 for first dc, working in ft lps only, dc in same st, 2 dc in ea st around to last st, sk last st, sl st in top of beg ch-3 = 30 dc.

Rnd 4: Sc in ea st around = 30 sc, sl st in first sc, turn.

Rnd 5 (wrong side): Ch 3, working in bk lps only, * (yo and pull up a lp) 5 times in next st, yo and through all lps on hook (puff made), ch 3, sk next st, rep from * around, ch 2, sl st in top of beg puff, turn = 15 puffs.

Rnd 6 (right side): Ch 1, sc in same st, sc in ea ch and puff around, sl st in first sc = 60 sc.

Rnd 7: Ch 5 for first dc and ch 2, working in ft lps only, (sk 1 st, dc in next st, ch 2) around, end with sl st in 3rd ch of beg ch-5 = 30 dc.

Rnd 8: Ch 1, working in bk lps only, sc in ea dc and ch around, sl st in first sc, turn = 90 sc.

Rnd 9 (wrong side): Ch 3, working in bk lps only, puff in same st, (ch 3, sk 2 sts, puff in next st) around, ch 3, sl st in top of beg puff, turn = 30 puffs.

Rnd 10 (right side): Ch 1, sc in same st, sc in ea puff and ch around, sl st in first sc = 120 sc.

Rnd 11: Ch 3 for first dc, working in ft lps only, dc in ea st around, sl st in top of beg ch-3.

Rnd 12: Ch 1, working in ft lps only, sc in ea dc around, sl st in first sc.

Rnd 13: Ch 5 for first dc and ch 2, working in ft lps only, sk 1 st, dc in next st, (ch 2, sk 1 st, dc in next st) around, ch 2, sl st in 3rd ch of beg ch-5 = 60 dc.

Rnd 14: Ch 1, working in bk lps only, sc in ea ch and dc around, sl st in first sc, turn = 180 sc.

Rnd 15 (wrong side): Ch 3, working in bk lps only, puff in same st, ch 2, sk 2 sts, (puff in next st, ch 2, sk 2 sts) around, sl st in top of beg puff, turn = 60 puffs.

Rnd 16 (right side): Ch 1, sc in ea puff and ch around = 180 sc.

Rnd 17: Ch 3 for first dc, working in both lps, dc in ea of next 7 sts, 2 dc in next st, (dc in ea of next 8 sts, 2 dc in next st) around = 200 dc, sl st in top of beg ch-3. Fasten off.

Tie (make 2): Work as for heart chair back.

Bath Set

Finished Size

Bath mat: Approximately 21½" x 18¼", not including edging.
Bath towel edging: 1½" x 26½".
Hand towel edging: 1¼" x 15½".
Washcloth edging: 1¼" x 14".

Materials (for 1 set)

Sportweight cotton (137-yd. ball): 7 aqua.
DMC or Anchor embroidery floss (8-yd. skein) see color key (on page 54).
Size 3 pearl cotton (16-yd. skein): 6 very light sky blue (A), 11 light turquoise (B).
Sizes #5 and #6 steel crochet hooks, or size to obtain gauge.
Size 5 pearl cotton (27-yd. skein): 4 light blue (A), 2 light turquoise (B) for bath towel edging; 1 each light terra cotta (A), light peach (B), and light peach pecan (C) for hand towel edging; 1 each very light sky blue (A), light turquoise (B) for washcloth edging.
Size #7 steel crochet hook.
Purchased bath towel, hand towel, and washcloth to match edgings.

Gauge

Bath mat: 15 sc and 18 rows = 2" with size #5 hook.

Directions

Bath mat: Row 1: With size #5 hook and aqua, ch 170, sc in 2nd ch from hook and ea ch across, ch 1, turn.

Rows 2-166: Sc in ea st across, ch 1, turn. Fasten off after row 166.

Cross-stitch: Working over 2 stitches, center design on mat and work according to chart (on page 54) with 12 strands of floss.

Edging: *Note:* Make an even number of lps for row 1. **Row 1:** With size #6 hook and A, (ch 5, dc in 5th ch from hook) 206 times or length required to fit around bath mat. Fasten off.

Row 2: Turn, join B with sl st in center ch of lp at end of row 1, (ch 5, sc in center ch of next lp) across. Fasten off.

Row 3: Turn, join A with sl st in center ch of ch-5 lp at end of row 2, ch 4 for first dc and ch 1, (dc, ch 1, dc, ch 1, dc) in same st, * ch 2, sc in center of next lp, ch 2, (dc, ch 1) 3 times in center ch of next lp, dc in same st (shell made), rep from * across. Fasten off.

Row 4: Do not turn, join B in 3rd ch of beg ch-4 of row 3, ch 1, sc in next ch-1 sp, ch 9, (sc, hdc, 8 dc) in 2nd ch from hook, dc in ea of next 5 ch of ch-9, hdc in ea of next 2 ch, sc in ea of next 2 ch, sc in same ch-1 sp as before, ch 1, sc in next ch-1 sp, * ch 4, 2 dc in 4th ch from hook, sc in first ch-1 sp of next shell, ch 1, sc in next ch-1 sp, ch 9, (sc, hdc, 2 dc) in 2nd ch from hook, drop last lp from hook, insert hook in 5th st from base on prev scroll, pick up dropped lp, work 6 dc in same st as last dc, 2 dc in ea of next 2 ch, dc in next ch, hdc in ea of next 2 ch, sc in ea of last 2 ch, sc in same ch-1 sp as before, ch 1, sc in next ch-1 sp, rep from * across. Fasten off.

Finishing: Slipstitch edging to bath mat, easing fullness around corners. Slipstitch ends together, matching pattern.

Bath towel edging: *Note:* Make an even number of lps for row 1. **Row 1:** With size #7 hook and A, (ch 5, dc in 5th ch from hook) 60 times or desired length. Fasten off.

Rows 2-4: Rep rows 2-4 of bath mat edging. Fasten off after row 4.

Finishing: Slipstitch edging to towel.

Hand towel edging: *Note:* Pat is a multiple of 6 sps plus 1 sp. **Row 1:** With size #7 hook and A, ch 150 or desired length. Dc in 6th ch from hook, (ch 1, sk next ch, dc in next ch) across. Fasten off. Turn. (Base ch of 150 = 73 sps across.)

Row 2: Join B with sl st in ch-1 sp at end of row 1, ch 1, sc in same sp, (ch 3, sk 2 sps, 5 dc in next sp, ch 3, sk 2 sps, sc in next sp) across, ch 6, turn.

Row 3: (Sc in ea of next 5 dc, ch 7) across, end with ch 3, dc in last sc. Fasten off. Turn.

Row 4: Join C with sl st in top of dc at end of row 3, ch 6, * sk next sc, sc in ea of next 3 sc, ch 5, (dc, ch 2, dc) in center ch of ch-7 lp, ch 5, rep from * across, end with ch 3, dc in center ch of ch-6 lp, ch 1, turn.

Row 5: Sc in same st, * ch 5, sk 1 sc, sc in next sc, ch 5, (dc, ch 3, sc in top of dc to make a picot) 3 times in next ch-2 sp, dc in same sp, rep from * across, end with ch 5, sc in last st. Fasten off.

Finishing: Slipstitch edging to towel.

Washcloth edging: *Note:* Make an even number of lps for row 1. **Row 1:** With size #7 hook and A, (ch 5, dc in 5th ch from hook) 34 times or desired length.

Rows 2 and 3: Rep rows 2 and 3 of bath mat edging. Fasten off after row 3.

Row 4: With wrong side facing and row 3 at bottom, join B with sl st in center of first row-1 lp. Ch 2, 3 dc in sp bet first and 2nd lps, ch 5, (3 dc in sp bet next 2 lps, ch 5) across, 3 dc bet last 2 lps, ch 2, sc in center of last lp, ch 6, turn.

Row 5: Dc in center st of first 3-dc grp, (ch 5, sl st in 5th ch from hook to make a picot, ch 1, dc in same dc, sc in next ch-5 lp, dc in center st of next 3-dc grp) across, ch-5 picot, dc in same dc, ch 2, sc in row-4 sl st. Fasten off.

Finishing: Slipstitch edging to washcloth.

Color Key

Note: The number of 8-yd. skeins required for each color is indicated in parentheses.

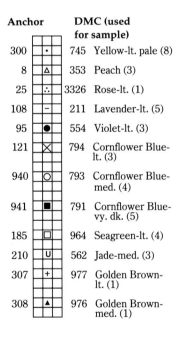

Anchor		DMC (used for sample)	
300	·	745	Yellow-lt. pale (8)
8	△	353	Peach (3)
25	∴	3326	Rose-lt. (1)
108	–	211	Lavender-lt. (5)
95	●	554	Violet-lt. (3)
121	✕	794	Cornflower Blue-lt. (3)
940	○	793	Cornflower Blue-med. (4)
941	■	791	Cornflower Blue-vy. dk. (5)
185	☐	964	Seagreen-lt. (4)
210	U	562	Jade-med. (3)
307	+	977	Golden Brown-lt. (1)
308	▲	976	Golden Brown-med. (1)

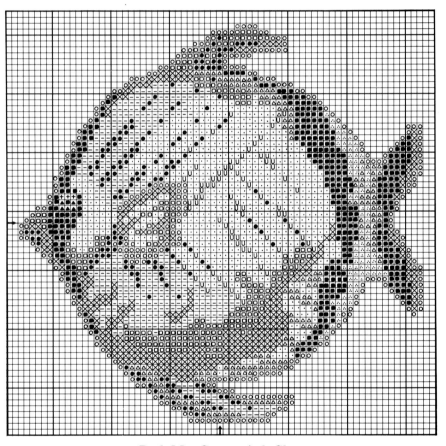

Bath Mat Cross-stitch Chart

Red Rose Doily

Red Rose Doily

Finished Size

Approximately 10" square.

Materials

Size 30 crochet cotton: 1 (250-yd.) ball each variegated red, variegated green; 2 (350-yd.) balls white.

Size #12 steel crochet hook, or size to obtain gauge.

Gauge

Rose = 3" diameter.

Directions

Rose: With variegated red, ch 6, join with a sl st to form a ring.

Rnd 1: Ch 1, 7 sc in ring, sl st in beg ch-1.

Rnd 2: Ch 5 for first dc and ch 2, (dc in next sc, ch 2) 7 times, sl st in 3rd ch of beg ch-5 = 8 sps around.

Rnd 3: Sl st in next sp, ch 1, (sc, 3 dc, sc) in ea sp around, sl st in first sc = 8 petals around.

Rnd 4: Holding petals to front of work, * ch 4, sc from back of work in next rnd-1 dc, rep from * around, sl st in base of beg ch-4.

Rnd 5: (Sc, 4 dc, sc) in ea ch-4 lp around, sl st in first sc.

Rnd 6: * Ch 5, sc bet next 2 petals as est, rep from * around, sl st in base of beg ch-5.

Rnd 7: (Sc, 6 dc, sc) in ea ch-5 lp around, sl st in first sc.

Rnd 8: * Ch 6, sc bet next 2 petals as est, rep from * around, sl st in base of beg ch-6.

Rnd 9: (Sc, 8 dc, sc) in ea ch-6 lp around, sl st in first sc.

Rnd 10: * Ch 7, sc bet next 2 petals as est, rep from * around, sl st in base of beg ch-7.

Rnd 11: (Sc, hdc, 2 dc, 4 tr, 2 dc, hdc, sc) in ea ch-7 lp around, sl st in first sc.

Rnd 12: * Ch 8, sc bet next 2 petals as est, rep from * around, sl st in base of beg ch-8.

Rnd 13: (Sc, hdc, 2 dc, 6 tr, 2 dc, hdc, sc) in ea ch-8 lp around, sl st in first sc.

Rnd 14: * Ch 9, sc bet next 2 petals as est, rep from * around, sl st in base of beg ch-9.

Rnd 15: (Sc, hdc, 2 dc, 8 tr, 2 dc, hdc, sc) in ea ch-9 lp around, sl st in first sc.

Rnd 16: * Ch 10, sc bet next 2 petals as est, rep from * around, sl st in base of beg ch-10.

Rnd 17: (Sc, hdc, 10 tr, 2 dc, hdc, sc) in ea ch-10 lp around, sl st in first sc. Fasten off.

Leaves: Join variegated green with a sl st in any rnd-15 sc bet petals, sc in same st, * ch 12, sc in 4th ch from hook, hdc in next ch, dc in ea rem ch, sc in first sc (leaf made), rep from * twice more to make 2 more leaves. Fasten off. (Sk sc bet next 2 petals, make 3 leaves as est in next sc bet 2 petals) 3 times = 4 grps with 3 leaves ea.

Edging: Rnd 1: Join white with a sl st in tip of any center leaf, sc in same st, ch 6, sc in tip of next leaf, * (ch 6, sc in 7th st of next petal, ch 6, sk 4 sts, sc in next st of petal) twice **, (ch 6, sc in tip of next leaf) 3 times, rep from * around, end last rep at **, ch 6, sc in tip of next leaf, ch 6, sl st in first sc.

Rnd 2: Ch 1, * 5 sc in next sp, sc in next sc, rep from * around, sl st in beg ch-1.

Rnd 3: Ch 12 for first dc and ch 9, dc in same st, * (ch 1, sk 1 st, dc in next st) 20 times, ch 1, sk 1 st, (dc, ch 9, dc) in next st for corner, rep from * around, sl st in 3rd ch of beg ch-12 = 21 sps bet corners.

Rnd 4: Sl st into corner sp, ch 4 for first tr, 7 tr in same ch-9 sp, * (sk next sp, 3 dc in next sp) to sp before next ch-9 corner, sk next sp, 8 tr in ch-9 corner, rep from * around, sl st in top of beg ch-4.

Rnd 5: Ch 4 for first tr, tr in same st, (ch 1, 2 tr in next tr) 7 times, * (3 dc in next sp, ch 1) 8 times, 3 dc in next sp, (2 tr in next tr, ch 1) 7 times, 2 tr in next tr, rep from * around, sl st in top of beg ch-4.

Rnd 6: Ch 6 for first tr and ch 2, (tr in next tr, ch 2) 14 times, tr in next tr, * (3 dc in next sp, ch 1) 7 times, 3 dc in next sp, (tr in next tr, ch 2) 15 times, tr in next tr, rep from * around, sl st in 4th ch of beg ch.

Rnd 7: Ch 7 for first tr and ch 3, (tr in next tr, ch 3) 14 times, * tr in next tr, (3 dc in next sp, ch 1) 6 times, 3 dc in next sp, (tr in next tr, ch 3) 15 times, rep from * around, sl st in 4th ch of beg ch.

Rnd 8: Ch 8 for first tr and ch 4, (tr in next tr, ch 4) 14 times, * tr in next tr, (3 dc in next sp, ch 1) 5 times, 3 dc in next sp, (tr in next tr, ch 4) 15 times, rep from * around, sl st in 4th ch of beg ch.

Rnd 9: Ch 9 for first tr and ch 5, (tr in next tr, ch 5) 14 times, * tr in next tr, (3 dc in next sp, ch 1) 4 times, 3 dc in next sp, (tr in next tr, ch 5) 15 times, rep from * around, sl st in 4th ch of beg ch.

Rnd 10: Ch 10 for first tr and ch 6, (tr in next tr, ch 6) 14 times, * tr in next tr, (3 dc in next sp, ch 1) 3 times, 3 dc in next sp, (tr in next tr, ch 6) 15 times, rep from * around, sl st in 4th ch of beg ch.

Rnd 11: Ch 11 for first tr and ch 7, (tr in next tr, ch 7) 14 times, * tr in next tr, (3 dc in next sp, ch 1) twice, 3 dc in next sp, (tr in next tr, ch 7) 15 times, rep from * around, sl st in 4th ch of beg ch.

Rnd 12: Ch 12 for first tr and ch 8, (tr in next tr, ch 8) 14 times, * tr in next tr, 3 dc in next sp, ch 1, 3 dc in next sp, (tr in next tr, ch 8) 15 times, rep from * around, sl st in 4th ch of beg ch.

Rnd 13: Ch 13 for first tr and ch 9, (tr in next tr, ch 9) 14 times, * tr in next tr, 3 dc in next sp, (tr in next tr, ch 9) 15 times, rep from * around, sl st in 4th ch of beg ch. Fasten off.

Rnd 14: Join white in center st of any 3-dc grp, sc in same st, ch 5, sl st in 5th ch from hook to make a picot, * ch 4, sc in next lp, ch-5 picot, ch 4, (sc in next tr, ch 5, sc in 3rd ch from hook, pull up a lp in ea of next 2 ch on ch-5 just made, yo and through all lps on hook, dc in sc just made, sc in next lp, ch 4, sc in same lp, ch-5 picot, ch 4) 14 times, sc in center st of 3-dc grp, ch-5 picot, rep from * around, sl st in first sc. Fasten off.

Slip Into Satin

Finished Size

Sheet edging: 69" x 9" (for twin-size sheet).
Pillowcase edging: 21" x 11" (for standard pillowcase).

Materials (for 1 sheet and 1 pillowcase)

Size 8 pearl cotton (95-yd. ball): 10 black.
Size #8 steel crochet hook, or size to obtain gauge.
Black sewing thread.
1,000 black bugle beads.
120 (⅜") black faceted teardrop beads.
120 (⅜") black faceted diamond beads.
120 black seed beads.
Beading needle.
Purchased black satin twin-size (flat) sheet and standard pillowcase.

Gauge

4 rows of band = 2".

Directions

Sheet edging: Ch 23.

Row 1: Dc in 8th ch from hook, ch 2, sk 2 ch, dc in next ch, ch 2, sk 2 ch, work a shell of (2 dc, ch 2, 2 dc) in next ch, (ch 2, sk 2 ch, dc in next ch) 3 times, turn.

Row 2: Ch 5 for first dc and ch 2, (dc in next dc, ch 2) twice, shell in ch-2 sp of shell, (ch 2, dc in next dc) twice, ch 2, sk 2 ch, dc in 3rd ch of tch, turn.

Rows 3-20: Rep row 2.

Row 21: Ch 5 for first dc and ch 2, (dc in next dc, ch 2) twice, shell in shell, (ch 2, dc in next dc) twice, ch 2, sk 2 ch, dc in 3rd ch of tch, do not turn, ch 17, working across side of band, sl st in top of last row-17 dc, sl st twice around post of same dc, sl st in top of next dc of band, ch 1, turn.

Row 22: Work 27 dc in ch-17 lp, work across band as est in row 2, turn.

Row 23: Work across band as est, do not turn, * ch 4, sk 3 dc, dc in ea of 3 dc, rep from * 3 times more, ch 4, sl st in top of last row-15 dc, sl st twice around post of same dc, sl st in top of next dc of band, ch 1, turn.

Row 24: Work a shell of * (3 dc, ch 2, 3 dc) in ch-4 sp, ch 1, rep from * 4 times more, work across band as est, turn.

Row 25: Work across band as est, do not turn, ch 5, (shell in shell, ch 5) 5 times, sl st in top of last row-13 dc, sl st twice around post of same dc, sl st in top of next dc of band, turn.

Row 26: Ch 3, working over and around prev ch-5 lp, sc in ch-1 sp of row 24, * ch 3, shell in shell, ch 3, sc around ch-5 lp in ch-1 sp of row 24 as est, rep from * 4 times more, ch 3, work across band as est, turn.

Row 27: Work across band as est, (ch 10, sc in shell) 5 times, ch 10, sl st in top of last row-10 dc, sl st twice around post of same dc, sl st in top of next dc of band, ch 1, turn.

Row 28: Work 12 dc in ea ch-10 sp, work across band as est, turn.

Row 29: Work across band as est, (ch 2, sk 1 dc, dc in next dc) 35 times, ch 2, sl st in top of last row-8 dc, sl st twice around post of same dc, sl st in top of next dc of band, ch 2, turn.

Row 30: (Dc in next dc, ch 2) across, work across band as est, turn.

Row 31: Work across band as est, * ch 5, sk 2 ch-sps, work a shell of (3 dc, ch 2, 3 dc) in next sp, rep from * 11 times more, ch 5, sl st in top of last row-6 dc, sl st twice around post of same dc, sl st in top of next dc of band, ch 6, turn.

Row 32: (Shell in shell, ch 6) 12 times, work across band as est, turn.

Row 33: Work across band as est, (ch 7, shell in shell) 12 times, ch 7, sl st in top of last row-4 dc, sl st twice around post of same dc, sl st in top of next dc of band, turn.

Row 34: Ch 4, working around ch-6 and ch-7 lps as est, sc in ch-5 lp of row 31, * ch 4, shell in shell, ch 4, sc around ch-lps in ch-5 lp of row 31 as est, rep from * 6 times more, ch 4, 3 dc in next shell, [ch 43, dc in 4th ch from hook and ea rem ch (long bar made), 3 dc in same shell, ch 4, sc around ch-lps in ch-5 lp of row 31 as est, ch 4, 3 dc in next shell] 4 times, ch 15, dc in 4th ch from hook and ea rem ch (short bar made), 3 dc in same shell, ch 4, sc around ch-lps in ch-5 lp of row 31 as est, ch 4, work across band as est, turn.

Rows 35-54: Work back and forth across band as est in row 2.

Rows 55-68: Rep rows 21-33.

Row 69: Ch 4, working around ch-6 and ch-7 lps, sc in ch-5 lp 2 rows prev, ch 4, 3 dc in next shell, sl st twice around post of st at end of short bar, 3 dc in same shell, * ch 4, sc around ch-lps in ch-5 lp as est, ch 4, 3 dc in shell, make long bar as est, 3 dc in same shell **, rep from * 3 times more, (ch 4, sc around ch-lps in ch-5 lp as est, ch 4, shell in shell) twice, rep from * to ** 4 times, ch 4, sc around ch-lps in ch-5 lp as est, ch 4, 3 dc in next shell, make short bar as est, 3 dc in same shell, sc around ch-lps in ch-5 lp as est, ch 4, sl st in last dc on next row of band, work across band as est.

Cont working pat as est for 69", or desired length. After completion of last scallop work 3 rows more on band. Fasten off. Weave inner 3 long bars bet scallops over and under ea other and tack tog at intersections (see photo).

Edging: Row 1: With right side facing, join thread in last dc 2 rows from end of band, (ch 8, shell in shell) 7 times, * (ch 8, sk 9 dc on long bar, shell in next dc on long bar) 3 times, ch 8, holding ends of outer long bars tog and working through both thicknesses, work shell in last st of both bars, (ch 8, sk 9 dc on long bar, shell in next dc on long bar) 3 times **, (ch 8, shell in shell) twice, rep from * across, end last rep at **, (ch 8, shell in shell) 7 times, sl st in last dc 2 rows from end of band, sl st twice around post of same dc, sl st in next dc of band, turn.

Row 2: * Ch 8, shell in shell, rep from * across, end with ch 8, sl st in last st on 2nd row from end of band, sl st twice around post of same dc, sl st in last dc of rem row of band, turn.

Row 3: * Ch 5, working around prev ch-8 lp,

sc in ch-8 lp of first edging row, ch 5, shell in shell, rep from * across, end with sl st in last dc of rem row of band. Fasten off.

Finishing: Tack ends of inner bars to outer bars at shells.

Secure black thread to edging band at beginning of first scallop. String 8 bugle beads and 1 teardrop bead. Tack teardrop bead to point of first scallop. String 8 bugle beads and 1 diamond bead with seed bead at tip of diamond bead. Tack diamond bead to point of next scallop. Repeat to string beads along length of edging.

Stitch edging to sheet on right side.

Pillowcase edging: *Note:* Pillowcase edging is worked in same manner as sheet edging except for 5 additional band rows before first scallop.

Row 1: Rep row 1 of sheet edging.

Rows 2-26: Rep row 2 of sheet edging.

Rows 27-40: Rep rows 21-34 of sheet edging.

Rows 41-60: Work back and forth across band as est in row 2.

Rows 61-73: Work as for sheet edging rows 21-33.

Row 74: Ch 4, working around ch-6 and ch-7 lps, sc in ch-5 lp 2 rows prev, ch 4, 3 dc in next shell, sl st twice around post of st at end of short bar, 3 dc in same shell, * ch 4, sc around ch-lps in ch-5 lp as est, ch 4, 3 dc in next shell, make long bar as est, 3 dc in same shell, rep from * 3 times more, (ch 4, sc around ch-lps in ch-5 lp as est, ch 4, shell in shell) 7 times, ch 4, sc around ch-lps in ch-5 lp as est, ch 4, sl st in last dc of next row on band, work across band as est. Do not fasten off. Weave inner 3 long bars bet scallops over and under ea other and tack tog at intersections (see photo).

Edging: Row 1: Work across band as est, (ch 8, shell in shell) 7 times, * ch 8, sk 9 dc on long bar, shell in next dc on long bar, rep from * twice more, ch 8, holding ends of outer long bars tog and working through both thicknesses, work shell in last st of both bars, (ch 8, sk 9 dc on long bar, shell in next dc on long bar) 3 times, (ch 8, shell in shell) 7 times, ch 8, sl st in last st on next row of band, sl st twice around post of same st, sl st in next dc of band, turn.

60

Row 2: * Ch 8, shell in shell, rep from * across, end with ch 8, sl st in last st of band, work across band as est, turn.

Row 3: Work across band as est, * ch 9, shell in shell, rep from * across, end with ch 9, sl st in last st of next row on band, sl st twice around post of same st, sl st in next dc of band, turn.

Row 4: * Ch 6, working around prev ch-8 and ch-9 lps, sc in ch-8 lp of first edging row, ch 6, shell in shell, rep from * across, end with ch 6, sl st in last st of band, work across band as est, turn.

Row 5: Work across band as est, (ch 12, sc in next shell) across, ch 12, sl st in last dc of next row of band, sl st twice around post of same dc, sl st in next dc of band, turn.

Row 6: Work 16 dc in ea ch-12 lp across, end with sl st in last st of band, work across band as est, turn.

Row 7: Work across band as est, dc in first st of 16-dc grp, * (ch 2, sk 1 dc, dc in next dc) 7 times, sk 1 dc, dc in first st of next 16-dc grp, rep from * across, ch 1, sl st in last st of next row on band, sl st twice around post of same dc, sl st in next dc of band, turn.

Row 8: * (Ch 2, dc in next dc) 7 times, dc in next dc, rep from * across, end with sl st in last st of band, work across band as est, turn.

Row 9: Work across band as est, dc in first dc, * ch 7, sk 3 ch-sps, work a shell of (3 dc, ch 2, 3 dc) in next sp, ch 7, sk 3 ch-sps, shell bet next 2 dc, rep from * across, end with ch 7, sk last 3 ch-sps, sl st in last st of rem row of band, sl st twice around post of same dc, sl st in corner of band, turn.

Row 10: (Ch 8, shell in shell) across, end with ch 8, sl st in last st of band, turn.

Row 11: * Ch 4, working over ch-8 lp, sc in ch-7 lp of row 9, ch 4, shell in shell, rep from * across, sl st in st at corner of band.

Rows 12-14: Rep rows 9-11, beg and ending in same corner sts of band. Fasten off.

Finishing: Finish as for sheet edging. If desired, tack teardrop and diamond beads to intersection points of woven bars.

Stitch edging to pillowcase on right side.

Dinnertime

Finished Size

Place mat: Approximately 16" x 21".
Napkin: Approximately 16" square.

Materials (for 1 place mat and 1 napkin)

½ yard (35"-wide) dress-weight linen.
Sewing thread to match.
Single-ply thick-and-thin natural silk (400-gr. cone): 1 ecru.
Size #5 steel crochet hook, or size to obtain gauge.

Gauge

3 shells = 2".

Directions

Outline 23 (2") squares on linen, leaving ½" between squares. Hemstitch along lines. Leaving ¼" seam allowance around each square, cut out squares.

Place mat (make 20 squares): **First square: Rnd 1:** Join yarn in any corner, ch 1, 2 sc in same corner, * sc evenly across edge to next corner = 15 sc across, 3 sc in corner, rep from * around, sc in beg corner, sl st in first sc.

Rnd 2: Ch 3 for first dc, 2 dc in same st for corner, * ch 5, sk 3 sts, 3 dc in next st for shell, (ch 5, sk 4 sts, 3 dc in next st) twice, ch 5, sk 3 sts, 3 dc in next st for corner, rep from * around, sl st in top of beg ch-3.

Rnd 3: Ch 1, sc in ea of next 2 dc, * (sc, ch 5, sc) in next sp, sc in ea of next 3 dc, rep from * around, sc in last dc, sl st in first sc. Fasten off.

2nd square: Rep rnds 1 and 2 as for first square.

Rnd 3 (joining rnd): Ch 1, sc in ea of next 2 dc, (sc in next sp, ch 2, sc in corresponding ch-5 lp on first square, ch 2, sc in same sp on 2nd square, sc in ea of next 3 dc) 4 times, * (sc, ch 5, sc) in next sp, sc in ea of next 3 dc, rep from * around, end with sc in last dc, sl st in first sc. Fasten off.

Cont to make and join squares as est for a row of 5 squares. Make 3 more rows of 5 squares ea. Join rows as est.

Napkin: Cut a 15" square of linen. Referring to diagram, cut 1 corner as shown. Hemstitch ¼" from edge all around linen.

Rnd 1: Join yarn in corner at short edge of napkin just beyond cutout area, sc evenly around napkin, sl st in first sc.

Rnd 2: Ch 3 for first dc, 2 dc in same st, (ch 5, sk 4 sts, 3 dc in next st) around napkin to beg of cutout area. Fasten off.

Square: Make 3 squares and join them in an L shape in same manner as for place mat.

Join L-shaped piece in cutout area of napkin as foll: Lay pieces on a flat surface with right sides up, sc in st at corner of cutout, * sc in corresponding ch-5 lp of joined squares, (sc in ea of next 6 sts on napkin, sc in next ch-5 lp on joined squares) 3 times, sc in ea st to within 1 st of corner of cutout. Dec across next 3 sts as foll: Bring up a lp in ea of next 3 sts, yo and pull through all lps on hook, sc in ea of next 6 sts on napkin, (sc in next corresponding ch-5 lp on joined squares, sc in ea of next 6 sts on napkin) 4 times, sc in ea st to next corner st on cutout, 3 sc in corner st, sc in ea of next 6 sts on napkin. Rep from * around rem edges of cutout and L-shaped piece. Fasten off.

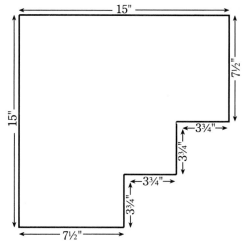

Napkin Cutting Diagram

Pansies Galore

Finished Size

Approximately 19½" x 46".

Materials

Sportweight cotton (115-yd. ball): 8 blue.
Size I afghan hook (10"-long), or size to obtain gauge.
Size F crochet hook.
Size 3 pearl cotton (16-yd. skein): 2 each of 7 colors for pansies; 1 each of 8 colors for pansies; 2 green for leaves; 1 each medium green, dark green for leaves.
Sizes #6 and #7 steel crochet hooks.
500 (¼"-diameter) blue glass beads.
Clear nylon thread.

Gauge

8 sts and 7 rows = 2" in afghan st.

Directions

Note: See page 141 for afghan st instructions.

Panel: With blue, ch 68, work 164 rows afghan st. Sl st in ea vertical bar across. Do not fasten off last lp.

Border: Rnd 1: Pick up lp with size F crochet hook, ch 1, * sc in ea st to next corner, (sc, ch 1, sc) in corner st, rep from * around, end with (sc, ch 1, sc) in beg corner, sl st in first sc.

Rnds 2-8: Ch 1, working in bk lps only, * sc in ea st to next corner, (sc, ch 1, sc) in corner ch-1 sp, rep from * around, sl st in first sc. Fasten off after rnd 8.

Large pansy (make 5): With size #6 hook and first color, ch 6, join with a sl st to form a ring.

Note: Use various colors of size 3 pearl cotton as desired to make pansies (see photo).

Rnd 1: Ch 3 for first dc, 2 dc in ring, (ch 8, 3 dc in ring) 4 times, ch 8, sl st in top of beg ch-3. Fasten off.

Rnd 2: Join next color with a sl st in center st of any 3-dc grp, ch 3 for first sc and ch 2, (11 dc in next lp, ch 2, sc in center dc of next grp, ch 2) 3 times, * (tr, ch 1) 11 times in next lp, tr in

same lp, ch 2, sc in center dc of next grp, ch 2, rep from * once more, sl st in base of beg ch-3. Fasten off.

Rnd 3: Join next color with a sl st in any ch-2 sp, (ch 3, sc bet next 2 sts) around, sl st in base of beg ch-3. Fasten off.

Medium pansy (make 15): With size #6 hook, ch 5, join with a sl st to form a ring.

Rnd 1: Rep rnd 1 of large pansy.

Rnd 2: Work as for rnd 2 of large pansy, except work only 9 dc or 10 tr in ch-8 lps.

Rnd 3: Rep rnd 3 of large pansy.

Small pansy (make 10): With size #7 hook, ch 5, join with a sl st to form a ring.

Rnds 1 and 2: Rep rnds 1 and 2 of medium pansy.

Rnd 3: Join next color with a sl st in any ch-2 sp, (ch 2, sc bet next 2 sts) around, sl st in base of beg ch-2. Fasten off.

Large leaf (make 16): *Note:* Use green, medium green, and dark green as desired to make leaves.

Row 1: With size #6 hook and green, ch 12, sc in 2nd ch from hook and ea of next 9 ch, 2 sc in last ch, working across opposite side of ch, sc in ea of next 10 ch, ch 1, turn.

Row 2: Sk first sc, working in bk lps only, sc in ea of next 9 sc, 2 sc in ea of next 2 sc, sc in ea of next 8 sc, ch 1, turn.

Row 3: Sk first sc, working in bk lps only, sc in ea of next 8 sc, 2 sc in ea of next 2 sc, sc in ea of next 8 sc, ch 1, turn.

Row 4: Sk first sc, sc in ea of next 8 sc, 2 sc in ea of next 2 sc, sc in ea of next 7 sc, ch 1, turn.

Row 5: Sk first sc, sc in ea of next 7 sc, 2 sc in ea of next 2 sc, sc in ea of next 7 sc. Fasten off.

Small leaf (make 4): Rep rows 1-3 of large leaf. Fasten off.

Finishing: Tack pansies and leaves to table runner as desired (see photo).

Attach beads to first round of border in every 4th stitch (about 1" apart). Attach a 2nd row of beads to last round of border in every other stitch.

Hats Off To You

Finished Size

Approximately 19" diameter.

Materials

7½ yards (45"-wide) floral print polished cotton fabric.

Sizes J and K crochet hooks, or size to obtain gauge.

4 (5" x 45") strips of green polished cotton fabric.

Sewing threads to match fabrics.

Gauge

Dc and ch 1 = 1" with size K hook.

Directions

Preparing fabric: Cut 100 (2½") strips across width of floral print fabric. With right sides facing and ¼" seam, stitch 2 strips together across 1 short edge. Repeat to stitch remaining floral strips together end to end to make 1 long strip. Press seams open.

Hat: With size J hook, ch 4, join with a sl st to form a ring.

Rnd 1: Ch 1, work 5 sc in ring.

Note: Work in a spiral and do not join. Use a safety pin to mark the beg of ea rnd.

Rnd 2: Work 2 sc in ea st around = 12 sts.

Rnd 3: Work 2 sc in ea st around = 24 sts.

Rnd 4: Work (2 sc in next st, sc in next st) around = 36 sts.

Rnd 5: Change to size K hook, (sc in next st, ch 1) around = 36 sc.

Rnd 6: Pull up a 1" lp, (dc in next sc, ch 1, sk 1 sp) around = 36 dc.

Rnd 7: Pull up a 1¼" lp, (dc in next sp, ch 2, dc in next sp, ch 1) around.

Rnd 8: * Dc in next ch-1 sp, (dc, ch 1, dc) in next ch-2 sp, rep from * around, turn.

Brim: Rnd 9: Working in rnds in ft lps only, ch 3 for first dc, dc in ea dc to next sp, (2 dc in sp, dc in ea dc) around, sl st in top of beg ch-3.

Rnd 10: Ch 4 for first dc and ch 1, (dc in next dc, ch 1) around, sl st in 3rd ch of beg ch-4.

Rnd 11: Ch 3 for first sc and ch 2, * sk 2 dc, (dc, ch 1, dc, ch 1, dc) bet last sk dc and next dc (shell made), ch 2, sk next 2 dc, sc in next dc, ch 2, rep from * around, end with sl st in first ch of beg ch-3.

Rnd 12: Ch 6, (sc in center dc of next shell, ch 5, sc in next sc, ch 5) around, end with sl st in first ch of beg ch-6.

Rnd 13: Ch 5 for first dc and ch 2, * (sc, ch 3, sc) in next lp, ch 2, dc in next sc, ch 2, rep from * around, end with sl st in 3rd ch of beg ch-5. Fasten off.

Finishing: With right sides facing and ¼" seam, stitch 2 green strips together across 1 short edge. Stitch remaining 2 green strips together in same manner. Cut 2 (5" x 45") strips from floral print. Stitch ends together in same manner. Press seams open. Along center 30" of each strip, fold under 1¼" on each long edge; then fold strip in half lengthwise. Finger press.

Braid 2 green strips and 1 floral strip together, beginning 29" from 1 end and ending 29" from other end. Wrap around hat and pin from inside. Tie ends of floral strips in a bow, leaving ends of green strips hanging for streamers.

Pins 'n Needles

Finished Size

Approximately 12" diameter.

Materials

Size 30 crochet cotton (563-yd. ball): 1 peach.
Size 20 crochet cotton (405-yd. ball): 1 ecru.
Size #12 steel hook, or size to obtain gauge.
¼ yard of rose velvet.
Sewing thread to match fabric.
Sawdust.
Seed beads: coral, peach.
Beading needle.

Gauge

Large flower = 1¾" diameter.
Small flower = 1" diameter.

Directions

Large flower (make 5): **First flower:** With peach, ch 8, join with a sl st to form a ring.

Rnd 1: Ch 7 for first dc and ch 4, dc in ring, (ch 4, dc in ring) 3 times, ch 4, sl st in 3rd ch of beg ch-4 = 5 sps, sl st into next sp.

Rnd 2: Ch 1, * (sc, 5 dc) in next sp, rep from * around, sl st in first sc.

Rnd 3: Holding petals to front of work, ch 6, (sc in back of next rnd-1 dc, ch 5) 4 times, sl st in first ch of beg ch-6.

Rnd 4: Ch 1, * (sc, 7 dc) in next sp, rep from * around, sl st in first sc.

Rnd 5: Ch 8, (sc bet next 2 petals as est, ch 7) 4 times, sl st in first ch of beg ch-8.

Rnd 6: Ch 1, * (sc, 2 dc, 6 tr, 2 dc) in next sp, rep from * around, sl st in beg ch-1.

Rnd 7: Ch 10, (sc bet next 2 petals as est, ch 9) 4 times, sl st in first ch of beg ch-10.

Rnd 8: Ch 1, * (sc, 2 dc, 8 tr, 2 dc) in next sp, rep from * around, sl st in beg ch-1.

Rnd 9: Ch 12, (sc bet next 2 petals as est, ch 11) 4 times, sl st in base of beg ch. Fasten off.

Rnd 10: Join ecru in last sl st, ch 1, * (sc, 2 dc, 11 tr, 2 dc) in next sp, rep from * around, sl st in beg ch-1. Fasten off.

2nd flower: Rep rnds 1-9 as for first flower.

Rnd 10 (joining rnd): Join ecru in last sl st, ch 1, * (sc, 2 dc, 11 tr, 2 dc) in next sp, rep from * 3 times more, (sc, 2 dc, 6 tr) in last sp, sl st in center st of any petal on first flower, (5 tr, 2 dc) in same sp on 2nd flower. Fasten off.

Rep rnds 1-10 to make a ring of 5 large flowers, sk 1 petal on prev flower to join successive flowers and rep rnd 10 of 2nd flower. Leave 1 petal of ea flower unattached on inside of ring and 2 petals unattached on outside of ring. Join 5th flower to first flower to complete the ring. Fasten off.

Center flower (make 1): Rep rnds 1-10 of first large flower, do not fasten off.

Rnd 11 (joining rnd): (Ch 5, sk 1 st, sc in next st) 8 times, place center flower inside 5-flower ring, sc in center st on unattached petal of any flower on ring, * (ch 5, sk 1 st, sc in next st of center flower) 8 times, sc in center st on unattached petal of next flower on ring, rep from * around, sl st in first ch of beg ch-5. Fasten off.

Small flower (make 10): With peach, ch 6, join with a sl st to form a ring.

Rnd 1: Ch 5 for first dc and ch 2, (dc in ring, ch 2) 6 times, sl st in 3rd ch of beg ch-5 = 7 sps.

Rnd 2: Ch 1, * (sc, 4 dc) in next sp, rep from * around, sl st in beg ch-1.

Rnd 3: Holding petals to front of work, ch 4, (sc in back of next rnd-1 dc, ch 3) around, sl st in first ch of beg ch-4.

Rnd 4: Ch 1, * (sc, 6 dc) in next sp, rep from * around, sl st in beg ch-1.

Rnd 5: Ch 6, (sc bet next 2 petals as est, ch 5) around, sl st in first ch of beg ch-6. Fasten off.

Rnd 6: Join ecru in any sp, ch 1, * (sc, 8 dc) in next sp, rep from * around, sl st in beg ch-1. Fasten off.

Referring to photo for positioning, tack small flowers to outside edge of 5-flower ring.

Edging: Rnd 1: Join peach in center st of center petal on any small flower. Ch 3 for first dc, 2 dc in same st, * ch 8, sc in center st of next petal, (ch 10, sc in center st of next petal) twice, ch 5, sc in center st of next petal on next large flower, ch 5, sc in center st of next petal on next small flower, ch 5, sc in prev ch-10 lp, ch 5, sc in center st of next petal on small flower, (ch 10, sc in center st of next petal) 4 times, ch 5, sc in center st of next petal on next large flower, ch 5, sc in center st of next petal on next small flower, ch 5, sc in prev ch-10 lp, ch 5, sc in center st of next petal on small flower, ch 10, sc in center st of next petal, ch 8, 5 dc in center st of next petal, rep from * around, end with 2 dc in same st as beg, sl st in top of beg ch-3.

Rnd 2: Ch 1, sc in same st, * (ch 5, 5 dc in next lp) twice, ch 5, dc in ea of next 2 lps, (ch 5, 5 dc in next lp) 3 times, ch 5, dc in ea of next 2 lps, (ch 5, 5 dc in next lp) twice, ch 5, sc in center st of 5-dc grp, rep from * around, end with sl st in first sc. Fasten off.

Rnd 3: Join ecru in ch-5 lp before last sl st, * (ch 5, sc in next lp, ch 5, sc in same lp, ch 5, sc in center st of next 5-dc grp) twice, (ch 5, sc in next lp, ch 5, sc in same lp) twice, (ch 5, sc in center st of next 5-dc grp, ch 5, sc in next lp, ch 5, sc in same lp) 3 times, (ch 5, sc in next lp, ch 5, sc in same lp, ch 5, sc in center st of next 5-dc grp) twice, ch 5, sc in next lp, ch 5, sc in same lp, rep from * around, end with sl st in first ch of beg ch-5. Fasten off.

Finishing: Use ½" seam. From velvet, cut a 12¼"-diameter circle for top and a 5½"-diameter circle for bottom.

Stitch rows of gathering threads ¼" and ½" from edge of 12¼" circle. Gather to fit bottom circle. With right sides facing and leaving a small opening, stitch top to bottom. Turn. Stuff firmly with sawdust. Slipstitch opening closed. Center crochet piece over top of pincushion. Tack center flower to pincushion. Pull small flowers around cushion to bottom circle and tack every other flower to pincushion at seam.

For each large flower, string 18 coral beads, coil, and tack to center of flower. For each small flower, string 8 coral beads, coil, and tack as above. Embellish flower petals with coral and peach beads as desired.

Mantel Elegance

Finished Size

Approximately 9½" x 64½".

Materials

Size 30 crochet cotton (150-yd. ball): 9 ecru.
Size #10 steel crochet hook, or size to obtain gauge.

Gauge

15 filet blocks and 12 rows = 2".
1 rep of chart = 21".

Directions

Row 1: Ch 70, dc in 6th ch from hook, (ch 1, sk 1 ch, dc in next ch) across = 33 sps, ch 4, turn.

Row 2: Sk 1 sp, dc in next dc, (ch 1, sk 1 sp, dc in next dc) across, ch 4, turn.

Row 3 (beg chart): Sk 1 sp, dc in next dc, (ch 1, sk 1 sp, dc in next dc) 24 times, (dc in next sp, dc in next dc) 3 times, (ch 1, sk 1 sp, dc in next dc) 5 times, ch 4, turn.

Rows 4-127: Cont foll chart as est. To work a filled sp over an open sp, dc in sp. To work a filled sp over a filled sp, dc in dc below. To work an open sp over an open sp, ch 1, sk 1 sp, dc in next dc. To work an open sp over a filled sp, ch 1, sk 1 dc, dc in next dc.

Rep rows 1-127 of chart as needed for desired length of swag. *Note:* Because chart has an odd number of rows, design will be reversed on 2nd rep.

Edging: Rnd 1: With right side facing and swag turned to work across short edge, join thread with a sl st corner, ch 6 for first dc and ch 3, 2 dc in same sp, * (2 dc in next sp) to next corner, (2 dc, ch 3, 2 dc) in corner, 2 dc in ea row across edge to next corner, (2 dc, ch 3, 2 dc) in corner, rep from * around, end with dc in same sp as beg, sl st in 3rd ch of beg ch-6, sl st into corner sp.

Rnd 2: Ch 6 for first dc and ch 3, 3 dc in same sp, * (ch 1, sk 1 st, dc in ea of next 3 sts) to next corner, ch 1, (3 dc, ch 3, 3 dc) in corner sp, rep from * around, end with 2 dc in same sp as beg, sl st in 3rd ch of beg ch-6, sl st into corner sp.

Rnd 3: Ch 6 for first dc and ch 3, 3 dc in same sp, * (ch 1, sk 3 dc, 3 dc in next sp) to next corner, ch 1, (3 dc, ch 3, 3 dc) in corner sp, rep from * around, end with 2 dc in same sp as beg, sl st in 3rd ch of beg ch-6, sl st into corner sp.

Rnd 4: Ch 6 for first dc and ch 3, dc in same sp, * (ch 1, dc in first st of next 3-dc grp, ch 1, dc in 3rd st of same grp) to next corner, ch 1, (dc, ch 3, dc) in center of corner ch-3 sp, rep from * around, sl st in 3rd ch of beg ch-6.

Rnd 5: Ch 4 for first tr, keeping last lp of ea st on hook, work 3 tr in same st, yo and through all lps on hook (beg cl made), ch 5, sk ch-3 sp, keeping last lp of ea st on hook, work 4 tr in next dc, yo and through all lps on hook (cl made), (ch 5, sk 1 dc, cl in next dc) around, adjust number of sk sts before corner as necessary to work a cl in first and last dc of ea corner, end with ch 5, sl st in top of beg cl.

Rnd 6: Sl st into corner sp, (sc, ch 3, sc) in corner sp, * (ch 1, dc in cl, ch 1, sc in next sp) to next corner, ch 1, (sc, ch 3, sc) in corner sp, rep from * around, end with ch 1, sl st in first sc.

Rnd 7: Sl st into corner sp, ch 6 for first dc and ch 3, dc in same sp, * (ch 1, dc in next sc, ch 1, dc in next dc) to next corner, ch 1, dc in next sc, ch 1, (dc, ch 3, dc) in corner sp, rep from * around, sl st in 3rd ch of beg ch-6.

Rnd 8: Ch 4 for first tr, beg cl in same st, ch 5, sk ch-3 sp, cl in next st, (ch 5, sk 1 dc, cl in next dc) around, end with ch 5, sl st in top of beg cl.

Rnd 9: Sl st into corner sp, (sc, ch 3, sc) in corner sp, * (ch 1, dc in cl, ch 1, sc in next sp) to next corner, ch 1, (sc, ch 3, sc) in corner sp, rep from * around, end with ch 1, sl st in first sc.

Rnd 10: Sl st into corner sp, ch 6 for first dc and ch 3, dc in same sp, * (ch 1, dc in next sc, ch 1, dc in next dc) to corner, ch 1, (dc, ch 3, dc) in corner sp, rep from * around, end with ch 1, sl st in 3rd ch of beg ch-6.

Rnd 11: Sl st into corner sp, ch 6 for first dc and ch 3, dc in same sp, * (ch 1, dc in next dc) to corner, ch 1, (dc, ch 3, dc) in corner sp, rep from * around, end with ch 1, sl st in 3rd ch of beg ch-6.

Rnd 12: Sl st into corner sp, ch 6 for first dc and ch 3, 2 dc in same sp, * (2 dc in next sp) to corner, (2 dc, ch 3, 2 dc) in corner sp, rep from * around, end with dc in same sp as beg, sl st in 3rd ch of beg ch-6.

Rnd 13: Sl st into corner sp, ch 6 for first dc and ch 3, dc in same sp, * ch 1, dc in next dc, (ch 1, sk 1 dc, dc in next dc) to corner sp, ch 1, (dc, ch 3, dc) in corner sp, rep from * around, end with ch 1, sl st in 3rd ch of beg ch-6.

Rnd 14: Sl st into corner sp, ch 3 for first dc, (dc, ch 3, 2 dc) in same sp, * work 2 dc in ea sp to next corner, (2 dc, ch 3, 2 dc) in corner sp, rep from * around, sl st in top of beg ch-3. Fasten off.

Oval cl: Row 1: With right side facing and swag turned to work across bottom edge, join thread with a sl st in top of 12th dc from corner (about 1" from end) ch 5, 4 tr in 5th ch from hook, ch 4, turn.

Row 2: Keeping last lp of ea st on hook, work 1 tr in ea of next 4 sts, yo and through all lps on hook, ch 1 to tighten (oval cl made). Fasten off.

Rep to make additional oval cl evenly spaced across bottom edge of swag (about 2" apart).

Lattice lps: Row 1: With right side facing and swag turned to work across bottom edge, join thread with sl st in corner sp, ch 16, dc in next oval cl, ch 16, sc in dc halfway bet oval cl) to next corner, sc in corner sp, ch 4, turn.

Row 2: Sk 1 ch, dc in next ch, * (ch 1, sk 1 ch, dc in next ch) 7 times, ch 1, (dc, ch 1, dc, ch 1, dc) in dc in oval cl (shell made), (ch 1, sk 1 ch, dc in next ch) 8 times, sk sc, dc in next ch, (ch 1, sk 1 st, dc in next ch) 7 times, ch 1, (dc, ch 1, dc) in next dc in oval cl), turn, ch 35, sl st in center dc of shell, turn, ch 4, sk 1 ch, dc in next ch, (ch 1, sk 1 ch, dc in next ch) 7 times, ch 1, sk 1 ch, shell in next ch, (ch 1, sk 1 ch, dc in next ch) 8 times, ch 4, sl st in same st as first ch of ch-35, (ch 1, dc) in same dc in oval cl **, (ch 1, sk 1 ch,

dc in next ch) 8 times, sk sc, dc in next ch, rep from * across, end last rep at **, (ch 1, sk 1 ch, dc in next ch) 7 times, ch 4, sl st in corner sp. Fasten off.

Tassels: For each tassel, cut 40 (16") strands. Fold strands in half. Cut 4 (19") pieces of thread. Tie 2 pieces around strands at fold. Knot remaining 2 pieces tightly around strands about 1" below fold. Referring to photo for positioning, tack tassels to lattice loops between oval clusters.

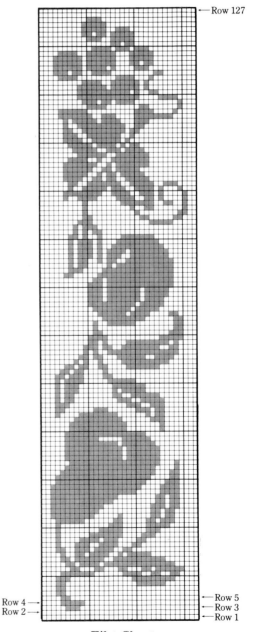

Filet Chart

Gifts & Frills

*For those times when
only a handmade gift will do,
this chapter is full
of novel ideas for unusual
crochet projects. In the
following pages, you're sure to
find the perfect pattern
for an extra-special treat
to give a friend or an
accessory to perk up
your own wardrobe.*

Pretty Pink Basket

Pictured on preceding pages.

Finished Size

Approximately 16" wide and 15" high, including handle.

Materials

Sportweight cotton (120-yd. ball): 4 pink.
Size #2 steel crochet hook, or size to obtain gauge.
Liquid fabric stiffener.
Empty cereal box covered with plastic wrap.
1 yard (1"-wide) pink taffeta ribbon with gold trim.
1 yard (⅝"-wide) variegated pink and green silk ribbon.

Gauge

4 shell sts = 3".
2 shell rows = 1".

Directions

Basket base: Ch 28. **Rnd 1:** Sc in 2nd ch from hook, sc in ea of next 26 ch, 3 sc in last ch, working back along opposite side of ch, sc in ea st to last st, 3 sc in last st.

Note: Work in bk lps only in a spiral for rnds 2-12. Use a safety pin to mark the beg of ea rnd.

Rnd 2: Sc in ea st to first st of 3-sc corner grp, (3 sc in first st of grp, sc in next st, 3 sc in next st), sc in ea st to next 3-sc corner grp, rep bet ( ) once.

Rnd 3: (Sc in ea st to next corner section, 3 sc in center st of 3-sc grp, sc in ea of next 3 sts, 3 sc in center st of next 3-sc grp) twice.

Rnds 4-12: Cont as est in rnd 3, working 3 sc in center st of ea 3-sc grp. At the end of rnd 12, sl st in first st.

Sides: Rnd 13: Ch 1, working through both lps, sc in ea st around, sl st in beg ch-1.

Rnds 14-18: Rep rnd 13.

Rnd 19: Ch 3 for first dc, (dc, ch 1, 2 dc) in same st (beg shell made), * (2 dc, ch 1, 2 dc) in next st (shell made), sk 3 sc, rep from * around, sl st in top of beg ch-3.

Rnd 20: Sl st into ch-1 sp of shell, ch 3 for first dc, 5 dc in same sp, drop lp from hook, insert hook in top of beg ch-3, pick up dropped lp and draw through, ch 1 to close (popcorn made), * ch 2, shell in ch-1 sp of next shell, ch 3, 6-dc popcorn in ch-1 sp of next shell, rep from * around, sl st in top of beg ch-3.

Rnd 21: Sl st into ch-1 of popcorn, ch 3 for first dc, beg shell in same st, * shell in ea shell and in ch-1 of ea popcorn around, sl st in top of beg ch-3.

Rnd 22: Sl st into ch-1 sp, ch 6 for first tr and ch 2, tr in same sp, (tr, ch 2, tr) in ea shell around, sl st in 4th ch of beg ch-6.

Rnd 23: Sl st into ch-2 sp, ch 3 for first dc, beg shell in same sp, shell in ea ch-2 sp around, sl st in top of beg ch-3.

Rnd 24: Sl st into ch-1 sp, ch 3 for first dc, beg shell in same sp, * ch 3, 6-dc popcorn in next shell, ch 2, shell in next shell, rep from * around, end with 6-dc popcorn in last shell, ch 2, sl st in top of beg ch-3.

Rnd 25: Sl st into ch-1 sp, ch 3 for first dc, beg shell in same sp, * shell in ch-1 of ea popcorn and in ea shell around, sl st in top of beg ch-3.

Rnd 26: Sl st into ch-1 sp, ch 7 for first tr and ch 3, tr in same sp, (tr, ch 3, tr) in ea shell around, sl st in 4th ch of beg ch-7.

Rnd 27: Sl st into ch-3 sp, ch 3 for first dc, (dc, ch 2, 2 dc) in same sp, (2 dc, ch 2, 2 dc) in ea ch-3 sp around, sl st in top of beg ch-3.

Rnd 28: Sl st into ch-2 sp, ch 3 for first dc, 5-dc popcorn in same sp, * ch 3, (2 dc, ch 2, 2 dc) in next ch-2 sp, ch 4, 6-dc popcorn in next ch-2 sp, rep from * around, end with (2 dc, ch 2, 2 dc) in last ch-2 sp, ch 4, sl st in top of beg ch-3.

Rnd 29: Sl st into ch-1 of popcorn, ch 3 for first dc, (dc, ch 2, 2 dc) in same st, * ch 1, (2 dc, ch 2, 2 dc) in next ch-2 sp and in ch-1 of next popcorn, rep from * around, end with (2 dc, ch 2, 2 dc) in last ch-2 sp, sl st in top of beg ch-3.

Rnd 30: Sl st into ch-2 sp, ch 7 for first tr and ch 3, tr in same sp, * ch 1, (tr, ch 3, tr) in next ch-2 sp, rep from * around, sl st in 4th ch of beg ch-7.

Rnd 31: Sl st into ch-3 sp, ch 3 for first dc, (dc, ch 3, 2 dc) in same sp, * ch 1, (2 dc, ch 3, 2 dc) in next ch-3 sp, rep from * around, sl st in top of beg ch-3.

Rnd 32: Sl st into ch-3 sp, ch 3 for first dc, (dc, ch 3, 2 dc) in same sp, * ch 3, 6-dc popcorn in next ch-3 sp, ch 2, (2 dc, ch 3, 2 dc) in next ch-3 sp, rep from * around, end with 6-dc popcorn in last ch-3 sp, ch 2, sl st in top of beg ch-3.

Rnd 33: Sl st into ch-3 sp, sc in same sp, ch 1, 4 tr in ch-1 of next popcorn, ch 3, sl st in top of prev tr to make a picot, 3 tr in same st (picot shell made), * ch 1, sc in next ch-3 sp, ch 1, picot shell in ch-1 of next popcorn, rep from * around, end with ch 1, sl st in first sc. Fasten off.

Handle (make 2): *Note:* Leave a 6" tail of yarn at beg.

Row 1: Ch 65, sc in 2nd ch from hook and ea ch across = 64 sc, ch 1, turn.

Row 2: Sc in ea st across = 64 sc.

Rows 3-6: Rep row 2. Do not fasten off.

Fold handle in half lengthwise, sl st end sts tog. Join edge of handle as foll: * ch 1, sk 1 st, sl st in next st working through both edges, rep from * across. Fasten off, leaving a tail.

Referring to photo for positioning, use tails of yarn to attach a handle to each side of basket.

Finishing: Following manufacturer's instructions, dip basket in fabric stiffener. Gently squeeze out excess.

Gently stretch and mold basket around box, matching bottom of box to bottom of basket. Pin all sides of basket to box about 5" from bottom. Gently shape handles and pin to sides of box. Pull remaining edges away from box slightly to shape basket (see photo). Let dry.

Weave 1"-wide ribbon through round-26 triple crochet stitches, leaving long tails at front. Make a multi-looped bow with ⅝"-wide ribbon. Knot 1"-wide ribbon tails around center of multi-looped bow to attach bow to front of basket.

Teddy T. Rags

Finished Size

Approximately 18" tall.

Materials

¼ yard each of 12 different cotton-polyester prints (3 yards of 45"-wide fabric).
Size G crochet hook, or size to obtain gauge.
Stuffing.
Carpet thread to match fabric.
2 (⅞") black shank buttons.

Gauge

4 sts and 4 rows = 1".

Directions

Choose a variety of fabrics. Use solids and prints in dark and light colors. Use fabrics that are printed through the entire fabric. Some fabric designs are stamped on 1 side only and the strips will twist as you crochet, showing the unprinted side as well as printed side.

Preparing fabric: Cut fabrics into ¼" strips. Do not tie all the strips together before you begin. Join a new strip as you approach the end of the strip being worked.

Head: Rnd 1: Ch 2, 6 sc in 2nd ch from hook.
Note: Work in a spiral. Use a safety pin to mark the beg of ea rnd.
   Rnd 2: Work 2 sc in ea sc around = 12 sts.
   Rnd 3: * Sc in ea of next 2 sts, 2 sc in next st, rep from * twice more, sc in ea of last 3 sts = 15 sts.
   Rnd 4: * Sc in ea of next 2 sts, 2 sc in next st, rep from * around = 20 sts.
   Rnd 5: (Sc in ea of next 3 sts, 2 sc in next st) around = 25 sts.
   Rnds 6 and 7: Sc in ea st around.
   Rnd 8: (Sc in ea of next 3 sts, 2 sc in next st, sc in ea of next 2 sts, 2 sc in next st) 3 times, sc in ea of next 3 sts, 2 sc in next st = 32 sts.
   Rnd 9: Sc in ea st around.
   Rnd 10: Work 2 sc in ea of next 8 sts, sc in ea of next 6 sts, 2 sc in ea of next 8 sts, sc in ea of next 10 sts = 48 sts. (Last 10 sts will be the chin.)
   Rnds 11-17: Sc in ea st around.
   Rnd 18: * Sc in ea of next 6 sts, pull up a lp in ea of next 2 sts, yo and through all lps (dec over 2 sts made), rep from * around = 42 sts.
   Rnd 19: (Sc in ea of next 5 sts, dec over next 2 sts) around = 36 sts.
   Rnd 20: (Sc in ea of next 4 sts, dec over next 2 sts) around = 30 sts.
   Rnds 21 and 23: Sc in ea st around.
   Rnd 22: (Sc in ea of next 3 sts, dec over next 2 sts) around = 24 sts.
   Rnd 24: (Sc in ea of next 2 sts, dec over next 2 sts) around = 18 sts. Stuff firmly.
   Rnd 25: (Sc in next st, dec over next 2 sts) around = 12 sts.
   Rnd 26: (Dec over next 2 sts) around = 6 sts. Fasten off, leaving a tail. Thread tail through rem sts, pull tightly and secure.

Body: Ch 24, join with a sl st to form a ring.
   Rnds 1 and 2: Sc in ea st around.
   Rnd 3: (Sc in ea of next 3 sts, 2 sc in next st) around = 30 sts.
   Rnds 4, 6, and 8: Sc in ea st around.
   Rnd 5: (Sc in ea of next 4 sts, 2 sc in next st) around = 36 sts.
   Rnd 7: (Sc in ea of next 8 sts, 2 sc in next st) around = 40 sts.
   Rnd 9: (Sc in ea of next 9 sts, 2 sc in next st) around = 44 sts.
   Rnd 10: (Sc in ea of next 10 sts, 2 sc in next st) around = 48 sts.
   Rnds 11 and 13: Sc in ea st around.
   Rnd 12: (Sc in ea of next 11 sts, 2 sc in next st) around = 52 sts.

Rnd 14: (Sc in ea of next 5 sts, 2 sc in next st) 6 times, sc in ea of 16 sts = 58 sts.

Rnds 15-22: Sc in ea st around.

Rnd 23: (Sc in ea of next 2 sts, dec over next 2 sts) around, sc in ea of last 2 sts = 44 sts.

Rnd 24: (Sc in ea of next 2 sts, dec over next 2 sts) 10 times, sc in ea of last 3 sts = 32 sts.

Rnd 25: (Sc in ea of next 3 sts, dec over next 2 sts) around, sc in ea of last 2 sts = 26 sts. Stuff firmly.

Rnd 26: (Sc in ea of next 2 sts, dec over next 2 sts) 6 times, sc in ea of last 2 sts = 20 sts.

Rnd 27: (Sc in next st, dec over next 2 sts) 6 times, sc in ea of last 2 sts = 14 sts.

Rnd 28: (Dec over next 2 sts) around = 7 sts. Fasten off, leaving a tail. Thread tail through rem sts, pull tightly and secure.

Leg (make 2): Ch 24, join with a sl st to form a ring.

Rnds 1-4: Sc in ea st around = 24 sts.

Rnd 5: (Sc in ea of next 10 sts, dec over next 2 sts) twice = 22 sts.

Rnd 6: Sc in ea st around.

Rnd 7: (Sc in ea of next 9 sts, dec over next 2 sts) twice = 20 sts.

Rnds 8-15: Sc in ea st around.

Rnd 16: (Sc in ea of next 8 sts, dec over next 2 sts) twice = 18 sts.

Rnd 17: Sc in ea st around.

Instep: Rows 1-4: Ch 1, turn, sc in ea of next 6 sts.

Foot: Rnd 1: Sc in side edge of ea of 4 instep rows, sc in ea of next 12 sts of leg, sc in side edge of ea of 4 instep rows, sc in ea of next 6 instep sts = 26 sts.

Rnds 2 and 3: Sc in ea st around.

Rnd 4: (Sc in ea of next 2 sts, dec over next 2 sts) 6 times, sc in ea of last 2 sts = 20 sts.

Rnd 5: * Dec over next 2 sts, sc in next st, rep from * to last 2 sts, dec over 2 sts = 13 sts.

Rnd 6: (Dec over next 2 sts) around, sc in last st. Fasten off, leaving a tail. Thread tail through rem sts, pull tightly and secure.

Arm (make 2): Ch 15, join with a sl st to form a ring.

Rnds 1-13: Sc in ea st around = 15 sts.

Rnd 14: (Sc in ea of next 4 sts, 2 sc in next st) around = 18 sts.

Rnds 15 and 16: Sc in ea st around.

Rnd 17: (Sc in next st, dec over next 2 sts) around = 12 sts.

Rnd 18: (Dec over next 2 sts) around = 6 sts. Fasten off, leaving a tail. Thread tail through rem sts, pull tightly and secure.

Ear (make 2): **Row 1:** Ch 9, sc in 2nd ch from hook and ea ch across = 8 sts, ch 1, turn.

Rows 2 and 3: Sc in ea st across, ch 1, turn.

Row 4: Dec over next 2 sts, sc in ea of next 3 sts, dec over next 2 sts, ch 1, turn.

Row 5: Sc in ea st across, working down side edge of ear, sl st in ea of 5 rows. Fasten off, leaving a tail to sew ear to head.

Finishing: Use carpet thread to assemble bear. Whipstitch head to body. Stuff legs and arms firmly. Whipstitch to body. Whipstitch ears to top of head. Sew buttons to face for eyes. Gather 3 fabric strips and tie a knot in 1 end. Braid the strips and knot end. Tie braided strips in a bow around bear's neck.

Three Pairs of Mittens

Three Pairs of Mittens

Finished Size

Each mitten is approximately 4½" wide and 11½" long.

Gauge

6 sts and 7 rows = 2".

Gray Mittens with Plum Trim

Materials

Worsted-weight wool-blend (150-yd. skein): 1 gray.

Worsted-weight acrylic (110-yd. ball): 1 plum.

Size I crochet hook, or size to obtain gauge.

Directions

Mitten (make 2): With gray, ch 22.

Row 1 (right side): Sc in 2nd ch from hook and ea ch across = 21 sts, turn.

Rows 2-4: Ch 1, sc in ea st across, turn. Drop gray.

Rows 5 and 6: Join plum, ch 1, sc in ea st across, turn. Fasten off plum after row 6.

Rows 7-10: Pick up gray, ch 1, sc in ea st across, turn.

Row 11: Ch 1, sc in ea of 2 sts, * 2 sc in next st, sc in ea of next 3 sts, rep from * across, sc in last st = 26 sts, turn.

Row 12: Ch 1, sc in ea st across, turn.

Row 13: Ch 1, sc in ea of next 11 sts, 2 sc in ea of next 2 sts, sc in ea rem st across = 28 sts, turn.

Rows 14 and 15: Ch 1, sc in ea st across, turn.

Row 16: Ch 1, sc in ea of next 11 sts, 2 sc in next st, sc in ea of next 2 sts, 2 sc in next st, sc in ea rem st across = 30 sts, turn.

Rows 17 and 18: Ch 1, sc in ea st across, turn.

Row 19: Ch 1, sc in ea of next 11 sts, 2 sc in next st, sc in ea of next 4 sts, 2 sc in next st, sc in ea rem st across = 32 sts, turn.

Row 20: Ch 1, sc in ea of next 11 sts, sk 8 sts (thumb), sc in ea rem st across = 24 sts, turn.

Rows 21-33: Ch 1, sc in ea st across, turn.

Row 34: Ch 1, * sc in ea of next 3 sts, pull up a lp in ea of next 2 sts, yo and through all lps (dec over 2 sts made), rep from * 3 times more, sc in ea rem st across = 20 sts, turn.

Row 35: Ch 1, (sc in ea of next 2 sts, dec over next 2 sts) 4 times, sc in ea rem st across = 16 sts, turn.

Row 36: Ch 1, * dec over next 2 sts, sc in ea of next 2 sts, rep from * twice more, dec over next 2 sts, sc in last st = 12 sts. Fasten off, leaving a tail of yarn. Thread tail through rem 12 sts, pull tightly and secure.

Thumb: Row 1: With right side facing, join gray in st before thumb hole, ch 1, sc in ea of next 9 sts = 10 sts, turn. (*Note:* Work thumb in rnds, if desired. Work in a spiral and use a safety pin to mark the beg of ea rnd.)

Rows 2-8: Ch 1, sc in ea st across = 10 sts, turn.

Row 9: (Dec over next 2 sts) across = 5 sts. Fasten off, leaving a tail of yarn. Thread yarn through rem 5 sts, pull tightly and secure. With gray, whipstitch thumb seam.

Trim: With right side facing and mitten turned to work down hand, join plum with sl st in corner of cuff, ch 2 for first sc and ch 1, sc in same st, * sc in ea st to other corner of cuff, (sc, ch 1, sc) in corner st, sc in ea st to beg ch-2, sl st in first ch of beg ch. Do not fasten off.

Assembly: Fold mitten in half with wrong sides facing. Working through both thicknesses, * ch 1, sl st in next st, rep from * across to close seam. Fasten off.

Green and Red Mittens

Materials

Worsted-weight wool-blend (150-yd. skein): 2 dark green.

Bulky-weight wool (105-yd. skein): 1 dark red.

Size I crochet hook, or size to obtain gauge.

Directions

Mitten (make 2): (*Note:* Use 2 strands of dark green held tog as 1. Use a single strand of dark red.) Work as for gray mitten, working colors as foll:

Rows 1-4: Dark green.
Rows 5-8: Dark red.
Rows 9-12: Dark green.
Rows 13-16: Dark red.
Rows 17-33: Dark green.
Rows 34-36: Dark red.

Thumb: Work as for gray mitten, working colors as foll:

Rows 1-7: Dark green.
Rows 8 and 9: Dark red.

Assembly: With right sides facing and leaving first 4 rows at cuff open, fold mitten in half and whipstitch seam with green yarn. Whipstitch thumb seam. Turn.

Cuff trim: Work in crab st (reverse sc) as foll: with right side facing, work even in sc from left to right instead of right to left.

Join dark red in st at edge of first row of cuff opening, crab st in ea of 4 rows of cuff opening, (crab st, ch 1, crab st) in st at corner of cuff, crab st in ea st around edge of cuff, (crab st, ch 1, crab st) in next corner st, crab st in ea of 4 rows of cuff opening, sl st in first st. Fasten off.

Wrist trim: Join dark red with sl st in any st on row 7, sc in same st, * ch 2, sc in next st, rep from * around mitten, end with sl st in first sc. Fasten off.

Green and Light Green Mittens

Materials

Worsted-weight wool-blend (150-yd. skein): 2 dark green, 1 light green.

Size I crochet hook, or size to obtain gauge.

Directions

Mitten (make 2): (*Note:* Use 2 strands of yarn held tog as 1.) With dark green, ch 21.

Row 1: Sc in 4th ch from hook, (dc in next st, sc in next st) across, sc in last st = 19 sts including beg ch-3. Drop dark green, do not turn.

Row 2: Join light green at opposite end of work in top of beg ch-3 of row 1, ch 1, (dc in sc, sc in dc) across to last st, sc in last st = 19 sts, pick up dark green and pull through last 2 lps of last sc, turn.

Row 3: With dark green, ch 3 for first dc, (sc in dc, dc in sc) across, drop dark green, do not turn.

Row 4: Pull light green through top of tch at beg of row 3, ch 1, (dc in sc, sc in dc) across, pull dark green through last 2 lps of last sc, turn.

Row 5: Rep row 3.
Row 6: Rep row 4. Fasten off light green.
Row 7: Rep row 3, turn.
Row 8: Ch 1, 2 sc in next st, sc in ea st across to last st, 2 sc in last st = 21 sts, turn.
Rows 9 and 10: Ch 1, sc in ea st across, turn.
Rows 11-16: Work as for gray mitten rows 11-16.
Rows 17-34: Work as for gray mitten rows 19-36.

Thumb: Rows 1-9: With dark green, work as for gray mitten.

Assembly: With right sides facing, whipstitch mitten and thumb seams with dark green. Turn.

Baby's Christening Gown

Finished Size

Edging: Approximately 3½" wide.

Materials

Size 30 crochet cotton (563-yd. ball): 1 white.
Size #12 steel crochet hook, or size to obtain gauge.
Purchased christening gown.
White sewing thread.

Gauge

11 dc = 1".
1 pat rep (rows 2-17) = 3".

Directions

Edging: Ch 31.

Row 1: Dc in 6th ch from hook, (ch 1, sk 1 ch, dc in next ch) 3 times, ch 1, sk 1 ch, dc in ea of next 8 ch, (ch 1, sk 1 ch, dc in next ch) 5 times, ch 4, turn.

Row 2: Dc in next dc, (ch 1, dc in next dc) 3 times, ch 2, sk ch-1 sp and next dc, dc in ea of next 6 dc, ch 2, sk next dc and ch-1 sp, (dc in next dc, ch 1) 4 times, dc in 3rd ch of tch, ch 4, turn.

Row 3: Dc in next dc, (ch 1, dc in next dc) 3 times, ch 4, sk ch-2 sp and 2 dc, dc in ea of next 2 dc, ch 4, sk 2 dc and ch-2 sp, dc in next dc, (ch 1, dc in next dc) 3 times, ch 1, dc in 3rd ch of tch, ch 4, turn.

Row 4: Dc in next dc, (ch 1, dc in next dc) 3 times, ch 2, sk 2 ch, dc in ea of next 2 ch, dc in ea of next 2 dc, dc in ea of next 2 ch, ch 2, sk 2 ch, dc in next dc, (ch 1, dc in next dc) 3 times, ch 1, dc in 3rd ch of tch, ch 4, turn.

Row 5: Dc in next dc, (ch 1, dc in next dc) 3 times, ch 1, sk 1 ch, dc in next ch, dc in ea of next 6 dc, dc in next ch, (ch 1, dc in next dc) 4 times, ch 1, dc in 3rd ch of tch, ch 4, turn.

Rows 6-8: Rep rows 2-4.

Row 9: Rep row 5, do not ch 4 or turn at end of row, work scallop down edge of band as foll: ch 8, sl st in st at end of row 8, sl st to end of row 7, turn.

Row 10: Work 15 dc in ch-8 lp, dc in row-9 dc, (ch 1, dc in next dc) 3 times, cont across band as est in row 2.

Row 11: Rep row 3, end with dc in last dc, do not ch 4 or turn, (ch 2, sk 2 dc, 2 dc in next dc) twice, (ch 2, sk 1 dc, 2 dc in next dc) twice, ch 2, sk 2 dc, 2 dc in next dc, ch 2, sk 2 dc, sl st in st at end of row 6, sl st to end of row 5, ch 3, turn.

Row 12: Work (2 dc in next dc, dc in next dc, ch 3) 5 times, dc in row-11 dc, (ch 1, dc in next dc) 4 times, cont across band as est in row 4.

Row 13: Rep row 5, end with dc in last dc, do not turn, (ch 4, dc in next dc, 2 dc in next dc, dc in next dc) 5 times, ch 4, sl st in st at end of row 4, sl st to end of row 3, ch 4, turn.

Row 14: Work (dc in next dc, 2 dc in ea of next 2 dc, dc in next dc, ch 4) 5 times, dc in row-13 dc, (ch 1, dc in next dc) 4 times, cont across band as est in row 2.

Row 15: Rep row 3, end with dc in last dc, do not turn, (ch 4, dc in ea of next 3 dc, ch 3, dc in ea of next 3 dc) 5 times, ch 4, sl st in st at end of row 2, sl st to end of row 1, ch 3, turn.

Row 16: Work * (2 tr in ch-3 sp, ch 5, sl st in 5th ch from hook to make a picot) 3 times, 2 tr in same sp, ch 3, sc in ch-4 sp, ch 3, rep from * 3 times more, (2 tr, ch-5 picot) twice in last ch-3 sp, 2 tr in same sp, ch 3, dc in row-15 dc, (ch 1, dc in next dc) 4 times, cont across band as est in row 4.

Row 17: Work (dc in next dc, ch 1) 4 times, sk 1 ch, dc in next ch, dc in ea of next 6 dc, dc in next ch, (ch 1, dc in next dc) 5 times, ch 4, turn.

Rep rows 2-17 of pat for desired length.

Finishing: Beginning at side seam, slipstitch edging to hem of christening gown. Match and slipstitch ends of edging together.

Finished Size

Each block is approximately 5".

Orange Block

Materials

Worsted-weight acrylic (253-yd. skein):
1 orange.
Sportweight acrylic (175-yd. ball): 1 yellow.
Sportweight wool (124-yd. ball): 1 red.
Size G crochet hook, or size to obtain gauge.
Stuffing.

Gauge

4 sc and 4 rows = 1".

Directions

Block: Row 1: With orange ch 19, sc in 2nd ch from hook and ea st across = 18 sts, turn.

Rows 2-18: Ch 1, sc in ea st across, turn. Do not fasten off. (First section made.)

Row 19: Join yellow with sl st, ch 1, drop yellow, sc across 17 sts with orange, turn.

Row 20: Ch 1, sc in ea of next 15 sts, drop orange, with yellow sc in ea of 2 sc, turn.

Rows 21-36: Cont as est working 1 fewer st with orange and 1 more st with yellow ea row. Do not fasten off. (2nd section made.)

Rows 37-54: Work in sc across 18 sts, changing colors as foll: 2 rows yellow, 2 rows orange, 2 rows yellow, 2 rows orange, 2 rows yellow. Fasten off yellow after row 46. Work 8 rows orange. Fasten off orange after row 54. (3rd section made.)

Rows 55-72: Join yellow with sl st in first st of last row. Work even in sc across 18 sts. Fasten off after row 72. (4th section made.)

Top: With right side facing and block turned to work across side edge of 4th section, join orange in corner.

Row 1: Ch 1, sc in ea st across 4th section of block = 18 sts, turn.

Rows 2-18: Ch 1, sc in ea st across = 18 sc. Fasten off after row 18.

Bottom: With wrong side facing and block turned to work across opposite side edge of 4th section, join orange in corner. (*Note:* Carry color not in use across the row by working over it with the next grp of sts.)

Row 1: With orange ch 1, sc in ea of next 2 sts, (join yellow and sc in ea of next 3 sts, with orange sc in ea of next 3 sts) twice, with yellow sc in ea of rem 3 sts, turn.

Row 2: Ch 1, sc in ea st across working colors as est in row 1, change to yellow on last st of row, turn.

Row 3: With yellow ch 1, sc in ea of next 2 sts, (with orange sc in ea of next 3 sts, with yellow sc in ea of next 3 sts) twice, with orange sc in ea of last 3 sts, turn.

Row 4: Ch 1, sc in ea st across working colors as est in row 3, change to orange on last st of row, turn.

Rows 5-18: Rep rows 1-4 alternating colors every 2 rows for checkerboard pat. Fasten off after row 18.

Assembly: Fold first and 2nd sections of block with wrong sides facing, join red at corner of fold, ch 1, working across folded edge, sc in ea st across. Rep across all folded edges of block.

Fold block with wrong sides of first and 4th sections facing, join red in corner, ch 1, sc in ea st across to join. Join top to block around rem 3 sides in same manner. Rep to join 2 edges of bottom to block. Stuff block. Join rem edge.

Checkerboard Blocks

Materials (for 2 blocks)

Sportweight wool (124-yd. ball): 1 each red, blue.
Sportweight acrylic (175-yd. ball): 1 yellow.
Sportweight acrylic-wool blend (150-yd. skein): 1 green.
Size G crochet hook, or size to obtain gauge.
Stuffing.

Gauge

4 sc and 4 rows = 1".

Directions

Block A: Row 1: With red, ch 19, sc in 2nd ch from hook and ea st across = 18 sts, turn.

Rows 2-18: Ch 1, sc in ea st across, turn. Do not fasten off. (First section made.)

Row 19: With red ch 1, sc in ea of next 5 sts, join blue and sc in ea of next 6 sts, with red sc in ea of next 6 sts, turn.

Rows 20-24: Rep row 19 working colors as est, turn. Change to blue on last st of row 24.

Row 25: With blue ch 1, sc in ea of next 5 sts, with red sc in ea of next 6 sts, with blue sc in ea of next 6 sts, turn.

Rows 26-30: Rep row 25 working colors as est, turn. Change to red on last st of row 30.

Rows 31-36: Rep rows 19-24. Fasten off red after row 36. (2nd section made.)

Rows 37-54: With blue ch 1, sc in ea st across, turn. (3rd section made.)

Rows 55-60: Rep rows 25-30. Change to red on last st of row 60.

Rows 61-66: Rep rows 19-24. Change to blue on last st of row 66.

Rows 67-72: Rep rows 25-30. Fasten off after row 72. (4th section made.)

Top: With right side facing and block turned to work across side edge of 4th section, join blue in corner.

Row 1: Ch 1, sc in ea of next 8 sts, drop blue (do not carry across row), join red and sc in ea of next 9 sts, turn.

Row 2: Ch 1, sc in ea of next 8 sts, drop red (do not carry across row), with blue sc in ea of next 9 sts, turn.

Rows 3-9: Rep rows 1 and 2 working colors as est, turn. (*Note:* On row 9, carry blue across to end of row.)

Row 10: Beg with blue and carrying red across row, ch 1, sc in ea of next 8 sts, drop blue (do not carry across row), with red sc in ea of next 9 sts, turn.

Rows 11-18: Ch 1, sc in ea st across working colors as est, turn. Fasten off after row 18.

Bottom: With wrong side facing and block turned to work across opposite side edge of 4th section, join blue in corner.

Rows 1-18: Rep rows 1-18 as for top. Fasten off after row 18.

Assembly: With blue, finish as for orange block.

Block B: Work as for block A, substituting green for red and yellow for blue. Use green for assembly.

Stripes Block

Materials

Sportweight acrylic (175-yd. ball): 1 each blue, white, yellow.
Sportweight acrylic-wool blend (150-yd. skein): 1 green.
Size I afghan hook, or size to obtain gauge.
Size H crochet hook.
Stuffing.

Gauge

7 sts and 7 rows = 2" in afghan st.

Directions

Note: See page 141 for afghan st instructions.

First 3 sections: With blue, ch 18, work 54 rows afghan st, sl st in ea vertical bar across. Fasten off.

4th section: Join white, work 18 rows afghan st, sl st in ea vertical bar across. Do not fasten off last lp.

Top: Working down side edge of prev section, draw up 18 lps, work 8 rows afghan st. Drop white and carry it up side of work. Join green, work 2 rows. Fasten off. With white, work 2 rows. Join yellow, work 2 rows. Fasten off. With white, work 4 rows. Fasten off.

Bottom: Working down opposite edge of 4th section, join white, draw up 18 lps, work 8 rows afghan st. Drop white and carry it up side of work. Join blue, work 2 rows. Fasten off. With white, work 1 row. Join green, work 4 rows. Fasten off. With white, work 3 rows. Fasten off.

Assembly: With yellow and crochet hook, finish as for orange block.

Bonny Barrettes

Bonny Barrettes

Finished Size

Each barrette is approximately 7" diameter.

Materials (for 6 barrettes)

Size 8 pearl cotton (95-yd. ball): 1 each white, ecru, variegated red, black, peach, yellow.

Size #10 steel crochet hook.

Spray fabric stiffener.

Sewing threads to match crochet threads.

Barrette hardware.

White barrette: clear seed beads; 8 (¼") ribbon roses.

Ecru barrette: 7 (3mm) light green beads; light green seed beads.

Variegated red barrette: 6 (3mm) pink beads; pink seed beads; burgundy seed beads.

Black barrette: 40 rhinestones.

Peach barrette: 80 (3mm) assorted ceramic ball beads.

Yellow barrette: rainbow seed beads; 12 assorted iridescent faceted beads.

Directions

Barrette (make 1 of ea color): Ch 6, join with a sl st to form a ring.

Rnd 1: Work 18 sc in ring, sl st in first sc.

Rnd 2: (Ch 6, sk 2 sc, sl st in next sc) around, sl st in first ch of beg ch-6 = 6 lps.

Rnd 3: * (Sc, hdc, 3 dc, hdc, sc) in next lp, rep from * around, sl st in first sc.

Rnd 4: Sl st in next hdc, ch 3 for first dc, dc in same st, ch 3, sk 3 dc, 2 dc in next hdc, (ch 3, 2 dc in first hdc of next grp, ch 3, 2 dc in next hdc of same grp) around, ch 3, sl st in top of beg ch-3.

Rnd 5: Sl st into next ch-3 sp, ch 3 for first dc, (dc, ch 3, 2 dc) in same sp, * ch 1, (2 dc, ch 3, 2 dc) in next ch-3 sp (shell made), rep from * around, end with ch 1, sl st in top of beg ch-3.

Rnd 6: Sl st into next ch-3 sp, ch 3 for first dc, 4 dc in same sp, (ch 1, shell in next ch-3 sp, ch 1, 5 dc in next ch-3 sp) around, end with shell in last ch-3 sp, ch 1, sl st in top of beg ch-3.

Rnd 7: Ch 4 for first dc and ch 1, dc in next dc, (ch 1, dc in next dc) 3 times, ch 1, * (2 dc, ch 3, 2 dc, ch 3, 2 dc) in next ch-3 sp, ch 1, (dc in next dc, ch 1) 5 times, rep from * around, end with (2 dc, ch 3, 2 dc, ch 3, 2 dc) in last ch-3 sp, ch 1, sl st in 3rd ch of beg ch-4.

Rnd 8: Sl st in ch-1 sp, (ch 5, sc in next ch-1 sp) 3 times, * ch 1, shell in next ch-3 sp, ch 3, shell in next ch-3 sp, ch 1, sk next ch-1 sp, sc in next ch-1 sp, (ch 5, sc in next ch-1 sp) 3 times, rep from * around, end with shell in next ch-3 sp, ch 3, shell in last ch-3 sp, ch 1, sl st in first ch of beg ch-5.

Rnd 9: Sl st into ch-5 lp, (ch 5, sc in next ch-5 lp) twice, * ch 1, shell in next ch-3 sp, 5 dc in next ch-3 sp, shell in next ch-3 sp, ch 1 **, sc in next ch-5 lp, (ch 5, sc in next ch-5 lp) twice, rep from * around, end last rep at **, sl st in first ch of beg ch-5.

Rnd 10: Sl st into center of ch-5 lp, ch 5, sc in next ch-5 lp, * ch 1, shell in next ch-3 sp, ch 1, sk 2 dc, (dc in next dc, ch 1) 5 times, shell in next ch-3 sp, ch 1 **, sc in next ch-5 lp, ch 5, sc in next ch-5 lp, rep from * around, end last rep at **, sl st in first ch of beg ch-5. Fasten off.

Petal section: Row 1: With right side facing, join with a sl st in ch-3 sp of next shell, ch 3 for first dc, (dc, ch 3, 2 dc) in same sp, ch 1, sk next ch-1 sp, (sc in next ch-1 sp, ch 5) 3 times, sc in next ch-1 sp, ch 1, shell in ch-3 sp of next shell, ch 3, turn.

Row 2: Shell in shell, ch 1, sc in next ch-5 lp, (ch 3, sc in next ch-5 lp) twice, ch 1, shell in next shell, ch 3, turn.

Row 3: Shell in shell, ch 1, sc in next ch-3 lp, ch 3, sc in next ch-3 lp, ch 1, shell in next shell, ch 3, turn.

Row 4: Shell in shell, ch 1, sc in next ch-3 lp, ch 1, shell in next shell. Fasten off.

Rep rows 1-4 in ea of 6 rnd-10 shells.

Edging: Rnd 1: With right side facing, join with a sl st in first dc of first shell at top edge of any petal, ch 3, 3 dc in ch-3 sp of same shell, * dc in ch-3 sp of next shell, ch 3, (dc, ch 3, 2 dc) around post of dc just made, (ch 3, shell in next ch-3 lp) twice, ch 3, shell in ch-3 sp of next rnd-10 shell at base of same petal, ch 1, sc in ch-5 lp bet petals, ch 1, shell in ch-3 sp of next rnd-10 shell at base of next petal, ch 3, shell in next ch-3 lp, ch 3 **, sc in first dc of next shell, ch 3, 3 dc in ch-3 sp of same shell, rep from * around, end last rep at **, sl st in beg sl st.

Rnd 2: Sl st into ch-3 lp, ch 6 for first dc and picot, sl st in 3rd ch from hook to make a picot, (dc in same ch-3 lp, ch 3, sl st in top of dc to make a picot) twice, * ch 2, sc in ch-3 sp of next shell, ch 2, (dc, ch-3 picot) 3 times in ch-3 sp of same shell (3-dc-picot grp made), (ch 2, sc in ch-3 lp bet shells, ch 2, 3-dc-picot grp in next shell) twice, ch 2, sc in next ch-3 lp, ch 2, (3 dc in next shell) twice, ch 2, sc in next ch-3 lp, ch 2, 3-dc-picot grp in next shell, ch 2, sc in next ch-3 lp, ch 2, 3-dc-picot grp in next ch-3 lp, rep from * around, end with sl st in 3rd ch of beg ch-6. Fasten off.

Finishing: Lightly stiffen each barrette with spray fabric stiffener.

Note: Refer to photos for placement of beads and trims.

For white barrette, gather center of crochet piece, overlapping petals. Whipstitch in back to secure. Tack ribbon roses to center as desired. String seed beads as desired to make various lengths. Loop beads and attach to center of barrette.

For ecru barrette, run a gathering thread around center motif and gather tightly. Arrange round-3 scallops to make a flower in center of barrette. Attach a 3mm green bead in each scallop of flower. Attach green seed beads, as desired.

For variegated red barrette, gather center and attach 3mm pink beads as for ecru barrette. String seed beads as desired to make various lengths. Loop beads and attach to center of barrette.

For black barrette, gather center of crochet piece, overlapping petals. Whipstitch in back to secure. Attach rhinestones as desired.

For peach barrette, fold 1 petal in half and tack edges together. Repeat with opposite petal. Gather center and whipstitch to secure. Make 8 loops of 10 beads each and attach to center of barrette.

For yellow barrette, with right sides facing, roll opposite edges to center. Gather center tightly and whipstitch in back to secure. String seed beads as desired to make various lengths. Loop beads and attach to center of barrette. Attach 7 iridescent faceted beads to center of barrette. String remaining iridescent beads and seed beads and attach to center of barrette.

Whipstitch crochet to barrette hardware.

91

Basket Lace

Materials

Large basket (see photo).
Size 30 crochet cotton (563-yd. ball): 2 ecru.
Size #7 steel crochet hook, or size to obtain gauge.
Gold metallic thread (1000m spool): 1 each light gold, medium gold.
3"-wide lightweight canvas strip.
Gold spray paint.
Low-temperature glue gun and glue sticks.
Liquid fabric stiffener.
2¼ yards of medium gold cord.
2 yards (⅛"-wide) pink satin ribbon.
10 yards (⅝"-wide) pink wired-edge ribbon.
5½ yards (1"-wide) sheer pink ribbon.
1 pearl cluster.
2¼ yards (¼"-wide) sheer pink ribbon.
2 yards (1"-wide) beige wired-edge ribbon.
10 dozen small pearls.
3 dozen medium pearls.
3 dozen silk leaves.
3 dozen large pearls.
3 dozen large iridescent beads.

Gauge

2 ch-links = 1".

Directions

Chain link (ch-link): Ch 4, tr in 4th ch from hook, * ch 4, tr bet ch and tr, rep from * for required number of ch-links as specified in pat.

Cluster (cl): Keeping last lp of ea st on hook, work specified number of sts in next st, yo and through all lps on hook.

Note: Before beg crochet lace, measure around rim of basket. Make 3½"-wide lace the same length as basket rim and 5"-wide lace twice the length of basket rim.

3½"-wide lace: With #7 hook and ecru, make 99 ch-links (or length required to reach around basket rim once). Always beg this pat with an odd number of ch-links.

Rnd 1: Ch 3, work a shell of (2 dc, ch 3, 2 dc) in ea link to end link, ch 3, sl st in beg ch of ch-links, ch 3, working down opposite side of ch-links, work a shell of (2 dc, ch 3, 2 dc) in ea link to end link, ch 3, sl st in base of beg ch-3.

Rnd 2: Work 3 sc in next ch-3 sp, ch 3, work a shell of (3 dc, ch 3, 3 dc) in ch-sp of ea shell to end of work, ch 3, 3 sc in ea of next 2 ch-3 sps, ch 3, 3-dc shell in ea shell to beg, ch 3, 3 sc in last ch-3 sp, sl st in first sc.

Rnd 3: Sc in ea of next 3 sc, 3 sc in next ch-3 sp, ch 6, sc in ch-sp of next shell, * ch 15, sk 1 shell, sc in ch-sp of next shell **, ch 3, dc bet next 2 shells, ch 3, sc in ch-sp of next shell, rep from * to last shell ending last rep at **, ch 6, 3 sc in next ch-3 sp, sc in ea of next 6 sc, 3 sc in next ch-3 sp, ch 6, sc in ch-sp of next shell, rep from * to beg of work ending last rep at **, ch 6, 3 sc in next ch-3 sp, sc in ea of next 3 sc, sl st in first sc.

Rnd 4: Sl st in ea of next 6 sc and ea of next 3 ch, ch 3, 2-dc cl in same st as prev sl st, * 19 sc in next ch-15 lp **, 2-dc cl in next dc, ch 3, sl st in same dc, ch 3, 2-dc cl in same dc, rep from * to end of work ending last rep at **, sk 2 ch, 2-dc cl in next ch, ch 3, sl st in same ch, sl st in ea of next 3 ch, sl st in ea of next 12 sc and ea of next 3 ch, ch 3, 2-dc cl in same st as prev sl st, rep from * to beg of work ending last rep at **, sk 2 ch, 2-dc cl in next ch, ch 3, sl st in same ch, sl st in ea of next 3 ch and ea of next 6 sc.

Rnd 5: Sl st in ea of next 9 sts, * ch 4, sl st in first st of 19-sc grp, (ch 3, 2-dc cl in same st, ch 3, 2-dc cl in 3rd ch from hook, sk 3 sc, sl st in next sc, ch 5, sk 2 sc, sl st in next sc) twice, sk 3 sc, sl st in next sc, ch 5, sk 2 sc, sl st in next sc, ch 3, 2-dc cl in same st, ch 3, 2-dc cl in 3rd ch from hook, sk 3 sc, sl st in last sc of 19-sc grp, ch 4 **, sl st in sl st bet next 2 cl, rep from * across, end last rep at **, sl st in base of last cl, sl st in

ea of next 18 sts, rep from * across, end last rep at **, sl st in base of last cl, sl st in ea of next 9 sts. Fasten off. Sl st ends of lace tog.

Ecru lace bow (make 1): With #7 hook and ecru, make 19 ch-links. Rep rnds 1–5 of 3½"-wide lace.

5"-wide lace: With #7 hook and ecru, make 176 ch-links (or number required to reach around basket rim twice).

Rnds 1 and 2: Rep rnds rnds 1 and 2 of 3½"-wide lace. Do not fasten off.

Row 1: Working in rows along 1 edge of piece, sl st into next ch-3 sp, (ch 7, sc in ch-sp of next shell) across to last shell, do not sc in ch-3 sp at end of piece, turn.

Row 2: (Ch 7, sc in next ch-7 lp) across to last ch-7 lp, ch 4, tr in row-1 sc at end of work, turn.

Row 3: (Ch 7, sc in next lp) across, ch 4, tr in center st of last lp, turn.

Row 4: Ch 4 for first tr, 2-tr cl in same st, (3-tr cl in center st of next lp, ch 5, 3-tr cl in same st) across, end with 3-tr cl in center st of last lp, turn.

Row 5: Ch 3 for first dc, dc in same cl, (ch 5, 3 dc in center st of next ch-5 sp) across, ch 5, 2 dc in last cl, turn.

Row 6: Ch 3 for first dc, (3 dc in center st of next ch-5 sp, ch 5) across, sc in tch, turn.

Row 7: Ch 3 for first dc, (dc in ea of next 3 dc, 3 dc in next ch-5 sp) across, dc in ea of last 3 dc and tch, turn.

Row 8: Ch 3 for first dc, dc in ea of next 3 sts, * keeping last lp of ea st on hook, work a dc in ea of next 2 sts, yo and through all lps on hook (dec over 2 sts made), dc in ea of next 4 sts, rep from * across, dc in tch. Fasten off.

Flowers: Row 1: Working along other edge of lace, join thread in ch-sp of first shell, sc in same sp, * ch 4, tr in 4th ch from hook (1 ch-link made), ch 4, 2-dc cl in 4th ch from hook, ch 3, sl st in same st as cl, (ch 3, 2-dc cl in same st, ch 3, sl st in same st) twice (3-petal flower made), make 1 ch-link, sc in ch-sp of next shell, make 2 ch-links, ch 4, 2-dc cl in 4th ch from hook, ch 3, sl st in same st, ch 4, 2-tr cl in same st, ch 4, sl st in same st, ch 3, 2-dc cl in same st, ch 3, sl st

94

in same st (large 3-petal flower made), make 2 ch-links, sk 1 shell, sc in ch-sp of next shell, rep from * across. Fasten off. Sl st ends of lace tog.

Gold lace bow (make 11): With #7 hook and 1 strand ea of light gold and medium gold threads held tog as 1, make 12 ch-links.

Rnd 1: Sl st into sp of ch-link just made, ch 3 for first dc, work a beg shell of (dc, ch 3, 2 dc) in same ch-link, * (2 dc, ch 3, 2 dc) in next link (shell made), rep from * to end link, work 3 shells in end link, working down opposite side of ch-links, make a shell in ea link to end link, work 2 shells in last link, sl st in top of beg ch-3, sl st into next ch-3 sp.

Rnd 2: Ch 3 for first dc, (2 dc, ch 3, 3 dc) in same sp, * (3 dc, ch 3, 3 dc) in ea ch-3 sp around, sl st in top of beg ch-3. Fasten off.

Finishing: Spray basket with gold paint. Lightly spray ecru crochet lace with gold paint. Let dry.

From canvas strip, cut a piece twice the length of the basket rim. Glue canvas strip around rim of basket, pleating to fit. Stiffen canvas with liquid fabric stiffener. Let dry. Spray basket and canvas with gold paint.

Glue straight edge of 5"-wide lace around rim of basket, folding lace into pleats of canvas and draping so that lace extends beyond edge of canvas (see photo). Glue 3½"-wide lace around inside top of basket, overlapping edges of canvas and 5"-wide lace by ½".

Cut 46" lengths from gold cord and ⅛"-wide ribbon and wind around basket handle, securing ends at each end of handle. Make a multi-looped bow with remaining cord. Make a multi-looped bow with remaining ⅛"-wide ribbon.

Fold ends of ecru crochet lace bow to meet in center and tack to secure. Gather center to make bow and secure.

Cut 4 (20") pieces from pink wired-edge ribbon and make 4 multi-looped bows. Attach a bow on each side at ends of basket handle. Cut a 52" length from pink wired-edge ribbon and make a multi-looped bow. Cut a 52" length from 1"-wide sheer ribbon and make a multi-looped bow. Referring to photo, attach multi-looped bows on top of each other on handle in the following order: cord, ⅛"-wide ribbon, wired-edge ribbon, sheer

ribbon, crochet lace bow. Attach pearl cluster to bows.

Cut 15 (5") lengths of (¼"-wide) sheer ribbon and tie each piece in a bow. Cut 9 (7") lengths of beige wired-edge ribbon and tie each piece in a bow. Lightly spray beige bows with gold paint. Let dry.

Cut 12 (12") lengths of (1"-wide) sheer ribbon. Make 12 double-looped bows. Gather center of each bow and secure. For each bow, string 10 small pearls, wrap around center of bow and tack to secure. Make gold crochet lace bows in same manner as ecru crochet lace bow.

To make a ribbon rose, cut a 5" length of pink wired-edge ribbon. With wrong side up, fold both ends of ribbon at a right angle (see diagram). Run a gathering thread across bottom edge of ribbon. Slightly gather ribbon and simultaneously wrap it in a circle to make a flower. Tack through lower edge of ribbon to secure (see diagram). Trim any excess ribbon. Repeat to make 44 more roses. Glue medium pearls inside ribbon roses as desired.

Glue bows, ribbon roses, silk leaves, remaining pearls, and beads to 5"-wide crocheted lace as desired (see photo).

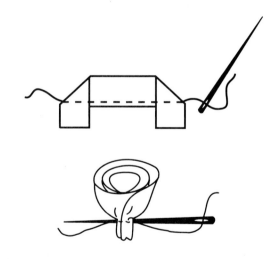

Ribbon Rose Diagram

Miniature Quartet

Heart

Materials

Size 70 tatting thread (5-gr. ball): 1 each peach, ecru.

Size #13 steel crochet hook.

Directions

With peach, ch 2, hdc in first ch (lp made).

Rnd 1: (Sc, hdc, 3 dc, hdc, 3 sc) in lp, ch 3, sl st in top of prev sc to make a picot, (3 sc, hdc, 3 dc, hdc) in lp, sl st in first sc.

Rnd 2: Ch 1, sc in next st, hdc in next st, 3 hdc in next st, 2 hdc in next st, hdc in ea of next 4 sts, 3 sc in picot (point of heart), hdc in ea of next 4 sts, 2 hdc in next st, 3 hdc in next st, hdc in next st, sc in next st, sl st in beg ch-1.

Rnd 3: Ch 3, sk 1 st, sl st in next st, (ch 3, sl st in next st) around to last 2 sts, ch 3, sk 1 st, sl st in last st, sl st in base of beg ch-3. Fasten off.

Rnd 4: Join ecru with sl st in same st as prev sl st, (ch 4, sc in next lp) around, end with ch 4, sl st in same st as beg, sc 2 rows down in center st at top of heart, pull tight to shape heart. Fasten off.

Pink Carnation

Materials

Size 70 tatting thread (5-gr. ball): 1 peach.
Size #13 steel crochet hook.

Directions

Ch 4, join with a sl st to form a ring.

Rnd 1: Ch 3 for first dc, 15 dc in ring, sl st in top of beg ch-3 = 16 sts.

Rnd 2: (Ch 6, sk next st, sc in next st) 7 times, ch 6, sk next st, sl st in base of beg ch-6, sl st into next lp.

Rnd 3: Ch 3 for first dc, 4 dc in same lp, * ch 3, 5 dc in next lp, rep from * 6 times more, ch 3, sl st in top of beg ch-3.

Rnd 4: Ch 3 for first dc, dc in ea of next 4 dc, (5 dc in next ch-3 sp, dc in ea of next 5 dc) 7 times, 5 dc in next ch-3 sp, sl st in top of beg ch-3.

Rnd 5: (Ch 3 for first dc, 4 dc in same st, sk next 4 sts, sl st in next st) 15 times, sl st in base of beg ch-3. Fasten off.

Crowned Star

Materials

Size 70 tatting thread (5-gr. ball): 1 ecru.
Size #13 steel crochet hook.

Directions

Ch 6, join with a sl st to form a ring.

Rnd 1: Ch 3 for first dc, 11 dc in ring, sl st in top of beg ch-3 = 12 sts.

Rnd 2: Ch 1, sc in next st, * ch 6, sc in 2nd ch from hook, hdc in next ch, dc in ea of next 2 ch, hdc in next ch, sc in ea of next 2 dc in ring, rep from * around, sl st in beg ch-1 = 6 petals.

Rnd 3: Ch 1, sc in ea of next 2 sts, * hdc in next st, dc in ea of next 2 sts, hdc in next st, 3 hdc in st at tip of petal, hdc in next st, dc in ea of next 2 sts, hdc in next st, sc in ea of next 3 sts, rep from * around, end with sc in last st, sl st in beg ch-1, sl st in ea st to tip of next petal.

Rnd 4: Ch 1, 2 sc in same st, (ch 8, 3 sc in st at tip of next petal) 5 times, ch 8, sl st in beg ch-1.

Rnd 5: Ch 6 for first dc and ch 3, sl st in 3rd ch from hook to make a picot, dc in same st, (dc, ch-3 picot, dc) in ea of next 2 sc, * ch 3, sk 2 ch, sc in ea of next 4 ch of ch-8 sp, ch 3, sk 2 ch, (dc, ch-3 picot, dc) in ea of next 3 sc, rep from * around, sl st in 3rd ch of beg ch-6. Fasten off.

Peach Petals

Materials

Size 70 tatting thread (5-gr. ball): 1 peach.
Size #13 steel crochet hook.

Directions

Ch 4, join with a sl st to form a ring.

Rnd 1: Ch 3 for first dc, dc in ring, (ch 3, 2 dc in ring) 5 times, ch 3, sl st in top of beg ch-3.

Rnd 2: * Ch 2, (sc, hdc, 5 dc, hdc, sc) in next ch-3 sp, rep from * around, sl st in base of beg ch-2.

Rnd 3: Sc in next ch-2 sp, ch 6, sc in same sp, * ch 5, sk sc and hdc, dc in ea of next 5 dc, ch 5, sk hdc and sc, (sc, ch 6, sc) in next ch-2 sp, rep from * around, sl st in first sc. Fasten off.

Wrapped in Style

Finished Size

Approximately 9" x 61", not including fringe.

Materials

Sportweight cotton-viscose (121-yd. ball): 8 black.

Size #0 steel crochet hook, or size to obtain gauge.

Worsted-weight wool-blend (98-yd. ball): 1 black with pink and aqua accents (A).

Sportweight linen with viscose thread (125-yd. ball): 1 black with pink, yellow, and blue viscose threads (B).

Bulky-weight translucent with metallic thread (132-yd. ball): 1 silver with gold and turquoise metallic threads (C).

Gauge

5 sc and 5 rows = 1".

Directions

Scarf: Row 1: With black, ch 45, sc in 2nd ch from hook and ea ch across, ch 1, turn.

Row 2: Sc in ea st across = 44 sc, ch 1, turn.

Rows 3-39: Rep row 2. At the end of row 39, do not ch 1. Turn.

Row 40: Ch 5 for first dc and ch 2, * sk 3 sts, keeping last lp of ea st on hook, work 5 dc in next st, yo and through all lps on hook (5-dc cl made) **, ch 4, rep from * 9 times more, end last rep at **, ch 2, dc in last st, turn.

Row 41: Ch 4 for first dc and ch 1, * 3 dc in next cl, ch 1, rep from * across, end with dc in 3rd ch of tch, ch 1, turn.

Row 42: Sc in first st (inc made), sc in ea dc and ch across to last st, 2 sc in last st = 44 sc. Fasten off, turn.

Row 43: Join A, ch 1, sc in ea st across, turn. Drop A.

Row 44: Join B, ch 4 for first tr, tr in ea of next 2 sts, dc in next st, hdc in next st, sc in ea of next 5 sts, hdc in next st, dc in ea of next 2 sts, tr in ea of next 4 sts, dc in ea of next 2 sts, hdc in next st, sc in ea of next 8 sts, hdc in next st, dc in ea of next 8 sts, hdc in next st, sc in ea of next 6 sts = 44 sts, turn. Drop B.

Row 45: Join C, ch 4 for first tr, tr in ea of next 3 sts, dc in ea of next 2 sts, hdc in ea of next 10 sts, dc in ea of next 2 sts, tr in ea of next 2 sts, dc in ea of next 4 sts, hdc in ea of next 10 sts, dc in next st, tr in ea of next 4 sts, dc in next st, hdc in ea of next 4 sts = 44 sts, turn.

Row 46: Ch 2 for first hdc, hdc in ea of next 4 sts, tr in ea of next 4 sts, dc in ea of next 2 sts, hdc in ea of next 9 sts, dc in ea of next 4 sts, tr in ea of next 2 sts, dc in next st, hdc in ea of next 11 sts, dc in ea of next 2 sts, tr in ea of next 4 sts = 44 sts, turn. Drop C.

Row 47: Pick up B, ch 1, sc in ea of next 14 sts, dc in ea of next 11 sts, sc in ea of next 8 sts, dc in ea of next 6 sts, sc in ea of next 4 sts = 44 sts, turn. Drop B.

Row 48: Pick up A, ch 1, sc in ea of next 8 sts, dc in ea of next 2 sts, tr in ea of next 6 sts, dc in next st, sc in ea of next 9 sts, dc in ea of next 2 sts, tr in ea of next 6 sts, dc in ea of next 2 sts, sc in ea of next 7 sts = 44 sts, turn. Drop A.

Row 49 (partial row): Pick up C, ch 2 for first hdc, hdc in ea of next 13 sts, drop C, turn.

Row 50: Pick up B in first st at end of row 48, ch 3 for first dc, dc in ea of next 3 sts, tr in ea of next 6 sts, dc in ea of next 2 sts, hdc in ea of next 5 sts dc in next st, tr in ea of next 8 sts, dc in next st hdc in ea of next 2 sts, hdc in side of last C st in partial row 49, carry C back across row, with B hdc in top of last st of row 49 and in ea of next 13 sts, turn. Fasten off C. Do not fasten off B.

Row 51: With B, ch 2 for first hdc, hdc in ea of next 17 sts, dc in ea of next 2 sts, tr in ea of next 8 sts, dc in ea of next 2 sts, hdc in ea of next 14 sts, turn. Drop B.

Row 52 (partial row): Join C, ch 2 for first hdc, hdc in ea of next 15 sts, drop C, turn.

Row 53: Pick up A in first st at end of row 51, ch 1, sc in ea of next 16 sts, dc in ea of next 5 sts, tr in ea of next 5 sts, dc in side of last C st in partial row 52, carry C back across row, with A dc in top of last st of row 51 and in ea of next 6 sts, sc in ea of next 9 sts = 44 sts, turn. Fasten off A and C.

Row 54: Pick up B, ch 3 for first dc, dc in ea of next 8 sts, hdc in ea of next 8 sts, sc in ea of next 4 sts, hdc in next st, dc in next st, tr in ea of next 6 sts, dc in ea of next 15 sts, turn. Fasten off.

Row 55: With black, sc in ea st across = 44 sc.

Rows 56-58: Rep rows 40-42.

Row 59: Sc in ea st across, ch 1, turn.

Rep row 59 until piece measures 47" from beg, or desired length.

Rep rows 40-58.

Rep row 59, 39 times. Fasten off after last rep.

Border: Join black with sl st in any corner, ch 1, * sc in ea st to next corner, (sc, ch 1, sc) in corner, rep from * around, end with (sc, ch 1) in beg corner, sl st in beg ch-1. Fasten off.

Fringe: Cut 132 (17") strands of black, 20 (17") strands of A, and 40 (17") strands of B. Gather 6 strands of black for plain tassel and 2 strands of A with 1 strand of B for mixed tassel.

Joining a tassel in every other stitch across each end of scarf and beginning at left-hand edge, knot a plain tassel in the first stitch. Knot tassels across each end of scarf as follows: 3 mixed tassels, 3 plain tassels, 2 mixed tassels, 5 plain tassels, 3 mixed tassels, 1 plain tassel, 2 mixed tassels, 2 plain tassels.

Finishing: Leaving a tail of yarn the same length as fringe at each end, weave strands over 2 single crochet stitches and under 2 single crochet stitches, except weave at ½" intervals over the pattern rows 40-58. Weave adjacent strands over and under opposite stitches.

With right side facing and beginning in first tassel at left-hand edge, weave 1 strand of C between first and 2nd stitches from edge to opposite end of scarf and out through tassel. Beginning in the next tassel, weave a strand of A between 3rd and 4th stitches from edge. Beginning in next tassel, weave a strand of A between 5th and 6th stitches. Beginning in 9th tassel, weave a strand of B between 15th and 16th stitches. Beginning in the same tassel, weave a strand of C between 16th and 17th stitches. Beginning in 15th tassel, weave a strand of B between 28th and 29th stitches. Beginning in the same tassel, skip 2 stitches and weave a strand of A. Beginning in next tassel, skip 1 stitch and weave a strand of C. Beginning in the same tassel, skip 1 stitch and weave a strand of C. Beginning in next tassel, skip 1 stitch and weave a strand of A. Beginning in the same tassel, skip 1 stitch and weave a strand of A. Beginning in 19th tassel, skip 5 stitches and weave a strand of A. Beginning in next tassel, skip 1 stitch and weave a strand of A. Beginning in the same tassel, skip 1 stitch and weave a strand of A. Trim fringe even.

Southwestern Tote Bag

Southwestern Tote Bag

Finished Size

Approximately 21" deep and 18" wide.

Materials

Fingering-weight mercerized cotton (184-yd. ball): 4 dark green; 1 each light green, turquoise, beige, mauve, pink.

Size E crochet hook, or size to obtain gauge.

Gauge

6 sc and 5 rows = 1".

Directions

Tote bag: With dark green, ch 4, join with a sl st to form a ring.

Rnd 1: Ch 1, 7 sc in ring, sl st in beg ch-1.

Note: Work in bk lps only in a spiral for rnds 2-94. Use a safety pin to mark the beg of ea rnd.

Rnd 2: Ch 1, 2 sc in ea st around = 16 sts.

Rnd 3: Sc in next st, (2 sc in next st, sc in next st) around, end with 2 sc in last st = 24 sts.

Rnd 4: (Sc in ea of next 2 sts, 2 sc in next st) around = 32 sts.

Rnd 5: Sc in next st, (2 sc in next st, sc in ea of next 3 sts) around, end with 2 sc in next st, sc in ea of last 2 sts = 40 sts.

Rnd 6: Sc in ea st around.

Rnd 7: (Sc in ea of next 4 sts, 2 sc in next st) around = 48 sts.

Rnd 8: Sc in ea of next 2 sts, (2 sc in next st, sc in ea of next 5 sts) around, end with 2 sc in next st, sc in ea of last 3 sts = 56 sts.

Rnd 9: Sc in ea of next 5 sts, (2 sc in next st, sc in ea of next 6 sts) around, end with 2 sc in next st, sc in last st = 64 sts.

Rnd 10: Sc in ea of next 3 sts, (2 sc in next st, sc in ea of next 7 sts) around, end with 2 sc in next st, sc in ea of last 4 sts = 72 sts.

Rnd 11: Sc in ea of next 6 sts, (2 sc in next st, sc in ea of next 8 sts) around, end with 2 sc in next st, sc in ea of last 2 sts = 80 sts. Fasten off.

Rnd 12: Join light green, sc in ea st around.

Rnd 13: Sc in ea of next 3 sts, (2 sc in next st, sc in ea of next 4 sts) around, end with 2 sc in next st, sc in last st = 96 sts.

Rnd 14: Sc in next st, (2 sc in next st, sc in ea of next 5 sts) around, end with 2 sc in next st, sc in ea of last 4 sts = 112 sts.

Rnd 15: Sc in ea of next 5 sts, (2 sc in next st, sc in ea of next 13 sts) around, end with 2 sc in next st, sc in ea of last 8 sts = 120 sts. Fasten off.

Rnd 16: Join turquoise, sc in ea st around. Fasten off.

Rnd 17: Join beige, sc in ea of next 7 sts, (2 sc in next st, sc in ea of next 14 sts) around, end with 2 sc in next st, sc in ea of last 7 sts = 128 sts.

Rnd 18: Sc in ea of next 4 sts, (2 sc in next st, sc in ea of next 7 sts) around, end with 2 sc in next st, sc in ea of last 3 sts = 144 sts. Fasten off.

Rnd 19: Join mauve, sc in ea of next 2 sts, (2 sc in next st, sc in ea of next 8 sts) around, end with 2 sc in next st, sc in ea of last 6 sts = 160 sts. Fasten off.

Rnd 20: Join pink, sc in ea st around.

Rnd 21: Sc in ea of next 6 sts, (2 sc in next st, sc in ea of next 9 sts) around, end with 2 sc in next st, sc in ea of last 3 sts = 176 sts. Fasten off.

Rnd 22: Join mauve, sc in ea of next 10 sts, (2 sc in next st, sc in ea of next 21 sts) around, end with 2 sc in next st, sc in ea of last 11 sts = 184 sts. Fasten off.

Rnd 23: Join beige, sc in ea of next 10 sts, (2 sc in next st, sc in ea of next 22 sts) around, end with 2 sc in next st, sc in ea of last 12 sts = 192 sts.

Rnd 24: Sc in ea of next 6 sts, (2 sc in next st, sc in ea of next 23 sts) around, end with 2 sc in next st, sc in ea of last 17 sts = 200 sts. Fasten off.

Rnd 25: Join turquoise, sc in ea st around. Fasten off.

Rnd 26: Join light green, sc in ea of next 12

sts, (2 sc in next st, sc in ea of next 24 sts) around, end with 2 sc in next st, sc in ea of last 12 sts = 208 sts.

Rnd 27: Sc in ea of next 8 sts, (2 sc in next st, sc in ea of next 25 sts) around, end with 2 sc in next st, sc in ea of last 17 sts = 216 sts.

Rnd 28: Sc in ea st around.

Rnd 29: Sc in ea of next 13 sts, (2 sc in next st, sc in ea of next 26 sts) around, end with 2 sc in next st, sc in ea of last 13 sts = 224 sts. Fasten off.

Rnd 30: Join dark green, sc in ea of next 7 sts, (2 sc in next st, sc in ea of next 13 sts) around, end with 2 sc in next st, sc in ea of last 6 sts = 240 sts.

Rnds 31-36: Sc in ea st around.

Rnds 37-81: Working according to chart, sc in ea st around, changing colors as indicated and carrying color not in use across by working over it. Fasten off only at the end of a rnd. Work pat over 20 sts and rep 11 times around = 12 pat. Fasten off all colors except pink after rnd 81.

Rnd 82: With pink, sc in ea st around. Fasten off.

Rnd 83: Join turquoise, sc in ea of next 7 sts, * pull up a lp in ea of next 2 sts, yo and through all lps (dec over 2 sts made), sc in ea of next 13 sts, rep from * around, end with dec over next 2 sts, sc in ea of last 6 sts = 224 sts. Fasten off.

Rnd 84: Join mauve, sc in ea of next 13 sts, (dec over next 2 sts, sc in ea of next 26 sts) around, end with dec over next 2 sts, sc in ea of last 13 sts = 216 sts.

Rnd 85: Sc in ea st around. Fasten off.

Rnd 86: Join turquoise, sc in ea of next 10 sts, (dec over next 2 sts, sc in ea of next 25 sts) around, end with dec over next 2 sts, sc in ea of last 15 sts = 208 sts. Fasten off.

Rnd 87: Join light green, sc in ea of next 7 sts, (dec over next 2 sts, sc in ea of next 24 sts) around, end with dec over next 2 sts, sc in ea of last 17 sts = 200 sts. Fasten off.

Rnds 88-94: Join dark green, sc in ea st around. At the end of rnd 94, sl st through both lps of first sc.

Rnd 95 (beading rnd): Working through both lps, ch 3 for first dc, dc in next st, (ch 2, sk 2 sts, dc in ea of next 2 sts) around, end with ch 2, sl st in top of beg ch-3.

Rnd 96: Ch 1, sc in next dc, 2 sc in next sp, (sc in ea of next 2 dc, 2 sc in next sp) around, end with sc in beg ch-1 = 200 sts.

Rnds 97-115: Working in a spiral through both lps, sc in ea st around. Fasten off after rnd 115.

Twisted cord drawstring: Cut 1 (78-yard) length of dark green. Fold end to end twice. Tie 1 end of folded yarn to blade of hand mixer, hold other end tightly, and turn mixer on low. Twist yarn tightly. Turn mixer off. Hold yarn tightly while removing from mixer blade. Fold yarn in half and let twist. Tie a knot in each end. Thread through beading row of bag. Knot ends together.

Color Key

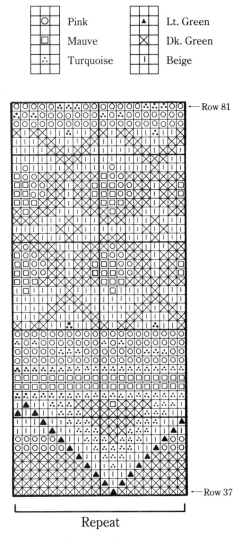

Pink
Mauve
Turquoise
Lt. Green
Dk. Green
Beige

←Row 81

←Row 37

Repeat

Crochet Chart

Beaded Scarf

Finished Size

Approximately 8" x 40", not including fringe.

Materials

Fingering-weight 3-ply hand-dyed cotton (40-yd. skein): 5 variegated purples and greens.

Size #7 steel crochet hook, or size to obtain gauge.

2mm beads, ¼" bugle beads, and seed beads in colors to complement yarn.

Black sewing thread.

Beading needle.

Gauge

5 cross sts = 2".
12 rows (3 pat rep) = 2½".

Directions

Separate 4 skeins of yarn into single-ply strands and make 12 balls. String a variety of 2mm, bugle, and seed beads on each ball. While crocheting, use approximately 6 beads randomly spaced across each row.

Scarf: Row 1: Ch 74, dc in 6th ch from hook, (ch 1, sk 1 ch, dc in next ch) across, turn = 36 dc.

Row 2: Ch 1, sc in first st, (sc in next ch, sc in next dc) across, end with sc in ea of 2 ch of tch, turn.

Row 3: Ch 1, * pull up a ½" lp, insert hook in next st, yo and pull through 1 lp, sl st in next st, ch 1, keep all lps on hook until last lp of row is worked, rep from * across, remove all lps except last lp of row, yo and pull through last lp, end with sl st in back lp of last st, turn = 36 lps.

Row 4: * Ch 1, sk first lp, insert hook in 2nd lp, yo and through both lps on hook, ch 1, insert hook in sk lp, yo and through both lps on hook (cross st made), rep from * across, end with sl st in top of last lp, turn.

Row 5: Ch 4 for first dc and ch 1, dc in sl st at top of next lp, (ch 1, sk ch-1 sp, dc in sl st at top of next lp) across, turn.

Rep rows 2-5 for pat until piece measures 40" from beg. Do not fasten off.

Border: Ch 1, * 3 sc in corner, sc in ea st to next corner, rep from * around, sl st in first sc. Fasten off.

Fringe: For each yarn tassel, cut 1 (8") strand of yarn. Knot a tassel in each stitch along 1 long edge of scarf.

For each bead tassel, secure black sewing thread to fringed edge of scarf. String a 3" length of assorted beads. Thread needle back through all beads except bottom bead, and secure thread at scarf edge. Attach bead tassels across fringed edge of scarf, as desired.

Lacy Throw

Finished Size

Approximately 60" x 90".

Materials

Size 10 crochet cotton (400-yd. ball): 36 ecru.

Size #10 steel crochet hook, or size to obtain gauge.

Gauge

Large motif = 5".

Directions

Large motif (make 216): **First motif:** Ch 8, join with a sl st to form a ring.

Rnd 1: Ch 5 for first dc and ch 2, (dc, ch 2) 7 times in ring, sl st in 3rd ch of beg ch-5.

Rnd 2: Ch 4 for first tr, keeping last lp of ea st on hook, work 2 tr in same st, yo and pull through all lps on hook (beg cl made), ch 3, * keeping last lp of ea st on hook, work 3 tr in next sp, yo and pull through all lps on hook (cl made), ch 3, cl in next st, ch 3, rep from * around, sl st in top of beg cl = 16 cl around.

Rnd 3: Ch 1, 5 sc in ea sp around, sl st in first sc.

Rnd 4: Ch 4 for first tr, beg cl in same st, * ch 5, sk 4 sts, dc in next st, ch 5, sk 4 sts, cl in next st, rep from * around, end with sl st in top of beg cl.

Rnd 5: Ch 11 for first dc and ch 8, * 6 dc in next sp, keeping last lp of ea st on hook, dc in same sp, dc in next sp, yo and pull through all lps on hook (dec made) **, 6 dc in same sp, ch 8, rep from * around, end last rep at **, 5 dc in same sp, sl st in 3rd ch of beg ch-11, sl st into ch-8 lp.

Rnd 6: Ch 7 for first tr and ch 3, (tr, ch 3) 4 times in same lp, tr in same lp (scallop made), * ch 3, dc in dec bet 6-dc grps **, (ch 3, tr) 6 times in next ch-8 lp, rep from * around, end last rep at **, ch 3, sl st in 4th ch of beg ch-7 = 8 scallops around.

Rnd 7: Ch 1, * (sc in next sp, ch 4, sl st in 4th ch from hook to make a picot, 2 sc in same sp) 5 times, 3 sc in ea of next 2 sps, rep from * around, sl st in beg ch-1. Fasten off.

2nd motif: Rep rnds 1-6 as for first motif.

Rnd 7 (joining rnd): Rep rnd 7 of first motif to last 2 scallops, (sc in next sp, ch-4 picot, 2 sc in same sp) twice, sc in next sp, ch 2, * sl st in corresponding picot on first motif, ch 2, sl st in top of sc just made on 2nd motif, 2 sc in same sp on 2nd motif, sc in next sp, ch 2, sl st in next picot on first motif, ch 2, sl st in top of sc just made on 2nd motif, 2 sc in same sp on 2nd motif **, (sc, ch-4 picot, 2 sc) in next sp on 2nd motif, 3 sc in ea of next 2 sps, (sc, ch-4 picot, 2 sc) in next sp, sc in next sp, ch 2, rep from * to ** once, (sc, ch-4 picot, 2 sc in next sp) twice, 3 sc in ea of next 2 sps, sl st in beg ch-1. Fasten off.

Cont to make and join motifs as est for a throw 18 motifs wide and 12 motifs long.

Small motif (make 187): *Note:* Small motifs are joined in the openings bet rows of large motifs.

Ch 8, join with a sl st to form a ring.

Rnd 1: Rep rnd 1 of large motif.

Rnd 2 (joining rnd): Ch 1, sc in next sp, ch 7, sl st in picot just beyond joining on large motif, * (ch 7, sc in side of prev sc, sc in same sp on small motif, sc in next dc, sc in next sp), ch 7, sk 2 picots on same large motif, sl st in next picot, rep bet ( ) once, ch 7, sk joining, sl st in next picot on next large motif, rep from * as est until small motif is joined to 4 large motifs in 8 picots, end with sl st in beg ch-1. Fasten off.

Treats & Tributes

*In this chapter, you'll find
a varied selection
of items designed with holiday
celebrations in mind. So, add a
little crochet spice to the
seasonal events in your life
by stitching a playful
jack-o'-lantern throw, a set of
shimmering Christmas
ornaments, or a patriotic
place mat.*

Patriotic Table Set

Pictured on preceding pages.

Finished Size

Place mat: Approximately 18½" x 13½".
Napkin: 18¼" square, including edging.
Napkin ring: 2" wide and 5½" around.

Materials (for 1 place setting)

Size 5 crochet cotton (141-yd. ball): 1 white.
Sportweight cotton (115-yd. ball): 1 each blue, red.
Size #6 steel crochet hook, or size to obtain gauge.
16½" square of white cotton fabric.

Gauge

1 shell and 1 popcorn = 1".
3 pat rows = 1".

Directions

Place mat: *Note:* Work ea row with right side facing.

Bottom edge: With blue, ch 144. **Row 1** (scallop edge): Keeping last lp of ea st on hook, work 2 dc in 4th ch from hook, yo and pull through all lps (2-dc bobble made), * ch 1, sk next 3 ch, sc in next ch, ch 3, 2-dc bobble in same ch, rep from * across = 35 scallops. Fasten off. Do not turn.

Row 2: Join red in top of beg ch-3 on row 1, ch 7, sl st in 4th ch from hook to make a picot, ch 2, 3-dc bobble in same st, * sc in next ch-3 sp, ch 5, sl st in 3rd ch from hook to make a picot, ch 2, 3-dc bobble in same sp, rep from * across, end with sc in last st. Fasten off.

Row 3 (beg stripes): With right side facing and piece turned to work across unworked side of base ch, join white in last st on row 1, sc in same st, (ch 3, sc in base of next bobble) across. Fasten off.

Row 4: Join white in first sc on prev row, ch 3 for first dc, 5 dc in ch-3 lp, drop last lp from hook, insert hook in first st of grp, pick up dropped lp and pull through (popcorn made), * ch 1, 5 dc in next ch-3 lp (shell made), ch 1, popcorn in next ch-3 lp, rep from * across, end with ch 1, dc in last st. Fasten off.

Row 5: Join white with sc in top of beg ch-3 on prev row, * ch 1, sc in ch-1 sp after popcorn, ch 5, sc in ch-1 sp after shell, rep from * across, end with ch 1, sc in last dc. Fasten off.

Row 6: Join white in first sc on prev row, ch 3 for first dc, * shell in ch-1 sp, ch 1, popcorn in ch-5 sp, ch 1, rep from * across, end with shell in last ch-1 sp, dc in last sc. Fasten off.

Row 7: Join red with sc in top of beg ch-3 on prev row, * ch 5, sc in ch-1 sp after shell, ch 1, sc in ch-1 sp after popcorn, rep from * across, end with ch 5, sc in last dc. Fasten off.

Row 8: Join red in first sc on prev row, ch 3 for first dc, * popcorn in ch-5 sp, ch 1, shell in ch-1 sp, ch 1, rep from * across, end with popcorn in last ch-5 sp, ch 1, dc in last sc. Fasten off.

Rows 9-29: Rep rows 5-8 for pat, working 4 rows ea with red and white for stripes (see photo).

Row 30: Rep row 6 with white.

Row 31 (beg star section): Join red in top of beg ch-3 on prev row, (ch 5, sc in ch-1 sp after shell, ch 1, sc in ch-1 sp after popcorn) 10 times. Fasten off. Join blue in last red sc, rep bet ( ) 7 times, ch 5, sc in last dc. Fasten off.

Row 32: Rep row 8 working colors as est in row 31.

Row 33: Join red and rep row 5 across to color change on prev row. Fasten off. Join white in last red sc and rep row 5 across rem sts. Fasten off.

Row 34: Rep row 6, work with red across red ch-lps and with blue across white ch-lps. Fasten off.

Row 35: Join white, rep row 7 across piece. Fasten off.

Rows 36-54: Cont as est, working 4 rows ea

110

with red and white for stripes, and working blue shells and popcorns, and white ch-lps for stars section. Fasten off.

Top edge: Row 55: With right side facing, join blue in top of beg ch-3 on row 54, ch 3, 2-dc bobble in same st, (ch 1, sc in top of last dc of shell, ch 3, 2-dc bobble in same st, ch 1, sc in next ch-1 sp after popcorn, ch 3, 2-dc bobble in same sp) across, end with ch 1, sc in top of last dc. Fasten off.

Row 56: Join red in top of beg ch-3 and rep row 2 above. Fasten off.

Side edge: With right side facing and mat turned to work across short edge, join white in corner, ch 3 for first dc, 5-dc popcorn in same st, * ch 1, shell in next dc, popcorn in next dc, rep from * across, end with ch 1, shell in last dc, ch 2, sc in corner of mat. Fasten off.

Rep side edge across rem short edge of mat. Fasten off.

Napkin: Turn edge of fabric under ⅛" twice for narrow hem. Press.

Rnd 1: Working over hemmed edge, join white with sc in any corner, 2 sc in same corner, * sc evenly across edge to next corner (inc or dec as necessary so there are 110 sts bet corner grps), 3 sc in corner, rep from * around, end with sl st in first sc. Fasten off.

Rnd 2: Join blue in center corner st, * ch 3, 2-dc bobble in same st, ch 1, sk 2 sts, sc in next st, ch 3, 2-dc bobble in same st, (ch 1, sk 3 sts, sc in next st, ch 3, 2-dc bobble in same st) across edge to 2 sts from corner, sk 2 sts, sc in corner st, rep from * around, end with sl st in base of beg ch-3. Fasten off.

Rnd 3: With red, rep row 2 of place mat. Fasten off.

Napkin ring: With white, ch 36, join with a sl st to form a ring.

Rnd 1: Ch 1, sc in ea ch around, sl st in first sc. Fasten off.

Rnd 2: Join blue in any sc, ch 3, 2-dc bobble in same st, (ch 1, sk 3 sts, sc in next st, ch 3, 2-dc bobble in same st) around, ch 1, sl st in base of beg ch-3. Fasten off.

Rnd 3: With right side facing and piece turned to work across unworked side of base ch, join red in same st as any 2-dc bobble, rep rnd 2. Fasten off.

White Christmas

Finished Size

Tree skirt: 62" diameter.
Stocking: 20" high.

Materials

8½ yards (45"-wide) white satin fabric.
White sewing thread.
Size 5 pearl cotton (53-yd. ball): 30 white for tree skirt; 3 white for stocking.
Size #7 steel crochet hook, or size to obtain gauge.
½ yard of batting.
2½ yards of small cording.
13" x 48" piece of white polyester organdy.
18" (½"-wide) white satin bias tape.
18" (½"-wide) white decorative trim.
2-yards-long string of small pearls.
White Balger blending filament.
30" (1"-wide) white taffeta ribbon.
4 yards of small white satin cord.

Gauge

Flower = 6¾" in diameter.

Directions

Tree skirt: Enlarge pattern and cut pieces as indicated on pattern. From satin, cut 2 (15½"-diameter) circles for yoke. Cut a 4"-diameter circle from the center of each 15½" circle. Cut across each yoke piece from outer edge to inner edge, to make an opening to fit around tree.

With wrong sides facing and raw edges aligned, turn under ¼" around edges of yoke pieces and baste together. Hemstitch ⅜" from edge all around yoke. Repeat to make 8 panels.

Note: Since the hemstitching may vary, inc or dec sc sts as necessary to get the required number of sts around ea of the 8 panels and around outer edge of yoke.

First panel: Rnd 1: With right side facing and panel turned to work across top edge, join pearl cotton with sc in corner, sc in same corner, 33 sc across top edge, 3 sc in corner, 125 sc across side edge, 3 sc in corner, 148 sc across bottom edge, 3 sc in corner, 125 sc across side edge, sc in beg corner, sl st in first sc.

Rnd 2: Ch 2 for first hdc, hdc in ea of next 5 sts, dc in ea of next 6 sts, tr in ea of next 6 sts, 6 tr in next st, drop last lp from hook, insert hook in first tr of grp, pick up dropped lp, draw through and tighten to close (popcorn made), ch 3, sc in top of popcorn to make a picot, tr in ea of next 6 sts, dc in ea of next 6 sts, hdc in ea of next 5 sts, (hdc, ch 2, hdc) in corner st, hdc in ea of next 6 sts, dc in ea of next 6 sts, tr in ea of next 6 sts, [(popcorn with picot in next st, tr in ea of next 3 sts, dc in ea of next 3 sts, hdc in ea of next 3 sts, sc in next st, hdc in ea of next 3 sts, dc in ea of next 3 sts, tr in ea of next 3 sts) 4 times, popcorn with picot in next st, tr in ea of next 6 sts, dc in ea of next 6 sts], hdc in ea st to corner st, (hdc, ch 2, hdc) in corner, hdc in ea of next 7 sts, * dc in next st, 2 dc in next st, dc in next st, tr in next st, 2 tr in next st, tr in next st, ch 1, popcorn with picot in next st, ch 1, tr in next st, 2 tr in next st, tr in next st, dc in next st, 2 dc in next st, dc in next st **, hdc in ea of next 3 sts, sc in next st, (ch 12, sk 6 sts, sc in next st) 3 times, hdc in ea of next 3 sts, rep from * 3 times more, end last rep at **, hdc in ea of next 7 sts, (hdc, ch 2, hdc) in corner st, hdc in ea of next 14 sts, dc in ea of next 6 sts, tr in ea of next 6 sts, rep bet [ ] once, hdc in ea of next 6 sts, hdc in same st as beg, ch 2, sl st in top of beg ch-2. Fasten off.

2nd panel: Rnd 1: Rep rnd 1 above.

Rnd 2: Rep rnd 2 above to work around 3 sides of 2nd panel. To work 4th side of 2nd panel, hdc in ea of 14 sts, dc in ea of next 6 sts, tr in ea of

113

next 6 sts, ch 1, popcorn in next st, join first and 2nd panels as foll: with both panels right side up and first panel beside unfinished edge of 2nd panel, ch 1, sl st in corresponding picot on first panel, ch 1, sc in top of popcorn on 2nd panel, ch 1, cont across edge of 2nd panel as for first panel, joining picots as est. Fasten off.

Cont as est to edge and join rem panels. To leave an opening to fit around tree, do not join first and last panels.

Edging: Row 1: With right side facing and skirt turned to work across bottom edge of ea panel, join thread with sl st in corner ch-2 sp, ch 6 for first dc and ch 3, (sk 2 sts, dc in next st, ch 3) 5 times, * (dc, ch 2, dc, ch 2, dc) in next picot (shell made), (ch 3, sk 2 sts, dc in next st) 4 times, (13 hdc in next ch-12 lp, sc in sc) 3 times, omit last sc of last rep, (dc in next st, ch 3, sk 2 sts) 4 times, rep from * twice more, shell in next picot, (ch 3, sk 2 sts, dc in next st) 5 times, ch 3, sk 1 st, dc in corner ch-2 sp. Fasten off.

Petal: With right side facing, join thread with sl st in first st of 13-hdc grp, (ch 6, sk 2 sts, sc in next st) 3 times, ch 3, sk 2 sts, dc in next st, turn, (ch 6, sc in next lp) twice, ch 3, dc in 3rd ch of next lp, turn, ch 6, sc in next lp, ch 3, dc in 3rd ch of next lp, turn, ch 3, dc in 3rd ch of next lp. Fasten off.

Work a petal in ea 13-hdc grp.

Row 2: With right side facing, join thread with sl st in 3rd ch of beg ch-6 (on row 1 of edging), ch 2 for first hdc, 3 hdc in ea of next 6 sps, * 2 hdc in next sp, hdc in center dc of shell, 2 hdc in next sp, 3 hdc in ea of next 4 sps, hdc bet dc and first hdc of 13-hdc grp, (4 hdc in ea of next 4 sps of petal, 3 hdc in st at point of petal, 4 hdc in ea of next 4 sps, sc in next sc) 3 times, omit last sc of last rep, hdc bet last hdc of grp and next dc, 3 hdc in ea of next 4 sps, rep from * across panel as est. Fasten off.

Rep edging across bottom edge of ea panel.

Yoke: With right side facing and yoke turned to work around inside edge, join thread with sc in corner at opening, sc in same corner, 84 sc around inside edge of yoke, 3 sc in corner, 35 sc across edge of opening, 3 sc in corner, 313 sc around outside edge, 3 sc in corner, 35 sc across edge

of opening, sc in beg corner, sl st in first sc. Fasten off.

Assembly: Lay yoke and panels with right sides up and openings aligned. Work across outside edge of yoke from opening around. Join thread with sl st in corner of yoke, ch 2 for first hdc, hdc in ea of next 5 sts, dc in ea of next 6 sts, tr in ea of next 6 sts, popcorn in next st, ch 1, sl st in corresponding picot at top edge of corresponding panel, ch 1, sc in top of popcorn on yoke, * (tr in ea of next 3 sts, dc in ea of next 3 sts, hdc in ea of next 3 sts, sc in next st, hdc in ea of next 3 sts, dc in ea of next 3 sts, tr in ea of next 3 sts, popcorn in next st), ch 2, sl st in corner st of first panel, ch 2, sl st in corner st of next panel, ch 2, sl st in top of popcorn on yoke, rep bet ( ), ch 1, sl st in picot on panel, ch 1, sc in top of popcorn on yoke, rep from * around as est, end with tr in ea of next 6 sts, dc in ea of next 6 sts, hdc in ea of next 6 sts to corner. Fasten off.

Flower (make 16): Ch 8, join with a sl st to form a ring.

Rnd 1: (Ch 8, sc in ring) 7 times, ch 5, dc in base of beg ch-8.

Rnd 2: Ch 1, (5 sc in next lp) 8 times, sl st in top of rnd-1 dc.

Rnd 3: Ch 3 for first dc, * dc in next sc, (ch 2, sk 1 st, dc in next st) twice, rep from * around, end with ch 2, sk 2 sts, sl st in top of beg ch-3.

Rnd 4: Ch 1, sc in next dc, * 2 sc in next sp, ch 3, 4 dc in next dc, ch 4, 2 sc in next sp, sc in ea of next 2 dc, rep from * around, sl st in beg ch.

Rnd 5: Ch 16 for first tr and ch 12, (tr in 3rd sc beyond 4-dc grp, ch 12) 7 times, sl st in 4th ch of beg ch-16.

Petal: Sl st in next ch-12 lp, * ch 2 for first hdc, 12 hdc in same lp, dc in last ch of same lp, turn, ch 6, sk 3 sts, sc in next st, (ch 6, sk 2 sts, sc in next st) twice, ch 3, dc in last st, turn, (ch 6, sc in next lp) twice, ch 3, dc in 3rd ch of next lp, turn, ch 6, sc in next lp, ch 3, dc in 3rd ch of next lp, turn, ch 3, dc in 3rd ch of next lp. Fasten off.

Work a petal in ea ch-12 lp around flower. Be sure all petals are worked with right side facing.

Rnd 6: Join thread with sl st in top of any

rnd-5 tr bet petals, ch 1, * 2 sc in side of hdc, 4 sc in ea of next 4 sps, 3 sc in st at point of petal, 4 sc in ea of next 4 sps, 2 sc in side of hdc, sc in top of next rnd-5 tr, rep from * around flower, end with sl st in beg ch. Fasten off.

Finishing: Referring to photo for placement, tack 8 flowers around skirt at intersection of panels and yoke and 7 flowers around bottom edge of skirt at intersection of panels. Tack half of last flower to edge of last panel.

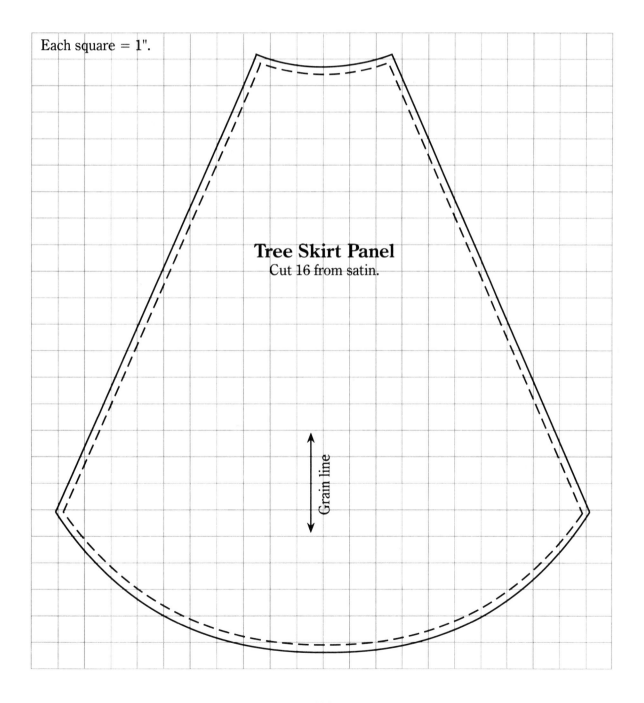

Each square = 1".

Tree Skirt Panel
Cut 16 from satin.

Grain line

Stocking: From satin, cut 2 (2¾" x 19") strips and 2 (3½" x 19") strips. With wrong sides facing and raw edges aligned, turn under ¼" around edges of 2¾" strips and baste together. Repeat with 3½" strips. Hemstitch ⅜" from edge along 1 long edge of 2¾" strip. Hemstitch ⅜" from edge along both long edges of 3½" strip. Fold each strip in half widthwise and stitch short ends together to form a tube. Press seams open. Stitch 2 (¼") tucks above hemstitching along bottom edge of 3½" strip.

Note: Since hemstitching may vary, inc or dec sc sts as necessary to obtain 120 sts on ea edge of cuff strips.

Cuff: Top strip: Work across hemstitched edge of 2¾" strip.
Rnd 1: Work 120 sc around, sl st in first sc.
Rnd 2: Ch 1, sc in same st, * hdc in ea of next 3 sts, dc in ea of next 3 sts, tr in ea of next 3 sts, popcorn with picot (as est in tree skirt, rnd 2 of first panel) in next st, tr in ea of next 3 sts, dc in ea of next 3 sts, hdc in ea of next 3 sts, sc in next st, rep from * around, end with sl st in first sc. Fasten off.

Bottom strip: Work across top edge of 3½" strip.
Rnd 1: Rep rnd 1 of top strip = 120 sc.
Rnd 2: Rep rnd 2 of top strip, joining to top strip at picots as foll: work rnd 2 to first picot, ch 1, sl st in corresponding picot on top strip, ch 1, sc in popcorn on bottom strip, cont around as est. Fasten off.
Work across bottom edge of 3½" strip.
Rnd 1: Rep rnd 1 = 120 sc.
Rnd 2: Ch 4 for first tr, * popcorn with picot in next st, tr in ea of next 2 sts, dc in ea of next 2 sts, hdc in ea of next 2 sts, sc in ea of next 2 sts, (ch 12, sk 4 sts, sc in next st) 3 times, hdc in ea of next 2 sts, dc in ea of next 2 sts, tr in ea of next 2 sts, rep from * around, sl st in top of beg ch-4.
Rnd 3: Sl st into next picot, ch 5 for first dc and ch 2, (dc, ch 2, dc) in same st, * (ch 2, sk 1 st, dc in next st) 4 times, (13 hdc in next ch-12 lp, sc in next sc) 3 times, end last rep with dc in sc, (ch 2, sk 1 st, dc in next st) 3 times, ch 2, (dc, ch 2, dc, ch 2, dc) in next picot (shell made), rep from *

around, end with sl st in 3rd ch of beg ch-5. Fasten off.
Petal: Work a petal in ea 13-hdc grp around as for petals on tree skirt edging.
Rnd 4: Join thread in center dc of any rnd-3 shell, ch 2 for first hdc, * 2 hdc in next sp, 3 hdc in ea of next 4 sps, hdc bet dc and first st of 13-hdc grp, (4 hdc in ea of next 4 sps, 3 hdc in st at point of petal, 4 hdc in ea of next 4 sps, hdc in next sc bet petals) 3 times, end last rep with hdc bet last hdc of grp and next dc, 3 hdc in ea of next 4 sps, 2 hdc in next sp, hdc in center dc of shell, rep from * around, end with sl st in top of beg ch-2. Fasten off.

Flower: Make 1 flower as for tree skirt.

Finishing: Use ¼" seam. Enlarge patterns and cut pieces from satin and batting as indicated on patterns. From satin, cut 1¼"-wide bias strips, piecing as needed to measure 2½ yards, and cut 1 (2" x 4") piece for hanger.
Make 2½ yards of corded piping. With raw edges aligned, stitch piping to each long edge on right side of stocking front.
Pin a batting stocking each to wrong sides of stocking front and back. With right sides facing and piping toward center, stitch stocking front to back along stitching line of piping. Trim batting from seam. With raw edges aligned, stitch piping around bottom edge on right side of stocking. Stitch sole to stocking along stitching line of piping. Clip curves and turn.
To make ruffle, stitch 13" ends of organdy together. Fold organdy in half lengthwise. Stitch rows of gathering threads through both layers, ¼" and ½" from raw edges. Mark a line around stocking, 4¼" from top edge. Slide ruffle over stocking. Align raw edge of ruffle with line and gather to fit. Stitch ruffle to stocking. Cover raw edge of ruffle with bias tape, topstitching along both edges of bias tape. Slide cuff over stocking, aligning raw edges and back seam. Pin. With raw edges aligned, stitch piping around top edge of stocking over cuff.
To make hanger, with right sides facing, fold 2" x 4" piece of satin in half lengthwise and stitch long edge. Turn. Fold in half and pin raw ends to top edge of stocking near back seam.

With right sides facing, stitch lining front to back along long edges, leaving opening in seam above heel. Insert sole and stitch. Do not turn. With right sides facing, slide lining over stocking, matching seams and raw edges. Stitch around top edge along stitching line of piping. Turn stocking through opening. Slipstitch opening closed. Tuck lining inside stocking. Slipstitch decorative trim around cuff ¾" below top edge. Tack an 18"-long pearl string along top edge of trim.

For each tassel, cut 220 (7") strands of crochet thread and 50 (7") strands of blending filament.

Fold strands in half. Tie a piece of thread around strands at fold. Wrap and knot another piece of thread tightly around strands 1" below fold. Make 4 tassels. Tack a tassel to each shell along bottom edge of cuff trim.

Tack crocheted flower to front of stocking above foot. Make a multi-looped bow from taffeta ribbon and tack to flower. Make a multi-looped bow from satin cord and tack to flower near taffeta bow. Knot ends of cord. Cut a 24"-long pearl string. Fold into loops and tack to cord bow. Repeat to tack a multi-looped satin cord bow and pearl string loops to top back of stocking.

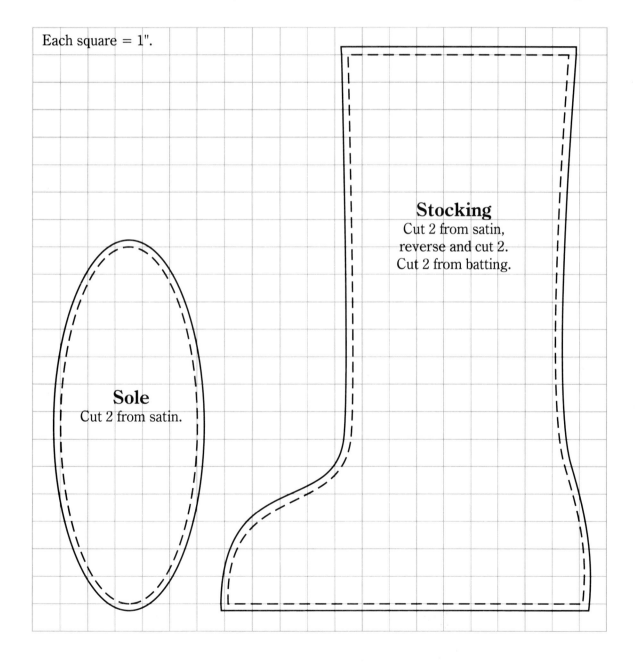

Each square = 1".

Sole
Cut 2 from satin.

Stocking
Cut 2 from satin, reverse and cut 2.
Cut 2 from batting.

Thanksgiving Plate Cover

Finished Size

Approximately 11" diameter.

Materials (for 1 plate cover)

Worsted-weight cotton (70-yd. skein): 2 brown, 1 green, 1 gold.

Size #0 steel crochet hook, or size to obtain gauge.

Gauge

5 dc = 1".

Directions

With brown, ch 6, join with a sl st to form a ring.

Rnd 1: Ch 5 for first dc and ch 2, (dc in ring, ch 2) 7 times, sl st in 3rd ch of beg ch-5.

Rnd 2: (Sc, dc, 2 tr, dc, sc) in ea sp around, sl st in first sc = 8 petals.

Rnd 3: Holding petals to front of work, * ch 5, sl st from back of work in next rnd-1 dc, rep from * around, sl st in base of beg ch-5.

Rnd 4: (Sc, dc, 3 tr, dc, sc) in ea ch-5 lp around, sl st in first sc.

Rnd 5: * Ch 6, sl st bet next 2 petals as est, rep from * around, sl st in base of beg ch. Fasten off.

Rnd 6: Join green with sl st in any ch-6 lp, ch 1, (sc, dc, 6 tr, dc, sc) in ea lp around, sl st in first sc. Fasten off.

Rnd 7: Join gold with sl st in 2nd tr of any rnd-6 petal, * ch 5, sc in 6th tr of same petal, ch 5, tr bet petals, ch 5, sc in 2nd tr of next petal, rep from * around, sl st in base of beg ch-5.

Rnd 8: Sl st in next ch-5 lp, ch 3 for first dc, (dc, ch 2, 2 dc) in same lp, (2 dc, ch 2, 2 dc) in ea ch-5 lp around, sl st in top of beg ch-3.

Rnd 9: Sl st into next ch-2 sp, * ch 5, sc in next ch-2 sp, rep from * around, ch 5, sl st in base of beg ch-5. Fasten off.

Rnd 10: Join brown with sl st in any ch-5 lp, ch 3 for first dc, (5 dc, ch 2, 6 dc) in same lp, (6 dc, ch 2, 6 dc) in ea ch-5 lp around, sl st in top of beg ch-3.

Rnd 11: Ch 3 for first dc, dc in ea of next 5 dc, * (2 dc, ch 3, 2 dc) in ch-2 sp, dc in ea dc to next ch-2 sp, rep from * around, sl st in top of beg ch-3. Fasten off.

Rnd 12: Join gold with sl st in any ch-3 sp, ch 3 for first dc, (dc, ch 3, 2 dc) in same sp, * ch 2, (2 dc, ch 3, 2 dc) in next ch-3 sp, rep from * around, end with ch 2, sl st in top of beg ch-3. Fasten off.

Rnd 13: Join green with sl st in any ch-3 sp, ch 3 for first dc, (2 dc, ch 3, 3 dc) in same sp, * ch 2, sc in next ch-2 sp, ch 2, (3 dc, ch 3, 3 dc) in next ch-3 sp, rep from * around, end with sl st in top of beg ch-3. Fasten off.

Rnd 14: With right side facing and holding scallops to front of work, join green with sl st in the back of any sc bet rnd-13 scallops, (ch 8, sc in the back of next sc) around, sl st in base of beg ch-8.

Rnd 15: Sl st into center of ch-8 lp, (ch 7, sc in next lp) around, sl st in base of beg ch-7.

Rnd 16: Sl st into center of ch-7 lp, (ch 6, sc in next lp) around, sl st in base of beg ch-6.

Rnd 17: Sl st into center of ch-6 lp, (ch 5, sc in next lp) around, sl st in base of beg ch-5. Fasten off.

Easter Delights

Finished Size

Each ornament is approximately 3" x 5".

Flower Ornament

Materials

Embroidery floss (8-yd. skein): 2 ecru; 1 each medium blue, light lavender, pink, medium lavender, blue, turquoise, purple.

Acrylic paints: light purple, medium purple.
Paintbrush.
Sizes #6 and #7 steel crochet hooks.
Finish coat gloss.
Plastic egg pantyhose container.
3 yards (1⁄16"-wide) purple ribbon.
26" (1⁄8"-wide) jade satin ribbon.
16 purple seed beads.
4 jade bugle beads.
Beading needle.

Directions

Note: To dye the ecru embroidery floss, wet the skein with clear water and squeeze out excess. With water, dilute each acrylic paint to the consistency of ink. Lightly paint the skein with each of the diluted paints, as desired. Blend the colors and vary the shades used for the best variegated effect. Turn the skein over and paint the other side, using the same colors in the same areas. Let dry.

Small flower: Make 2 small flowers working colors as specified. Use 3 strands of floss. For first small flower, use medium blue for A, light lavender for B, and pink for C. For 2nd small flower, use medium lavender for A, blue for B, and turquoise for C.

With size #7 hook and A, ch 6, join with a sl st to form a ring.

Rnd 1: Ch 1, 15 sc in ring, sl st in beg ch-1.

Rnd 2: Working in ft lps only, ch 2, (sc in next st, ch 1) around, sl st in first ch of beg ch-2. Fasten off.

Rnd 3: Working in rnd-1 bk lps only, join B with a sl st in any st, ch 1, work 2 sc in ea st around, sl st in beg ch-1 = 30 sts.

Rnd 4: Working in ft lps only, ch 3 for first dc, * hdc in next st, sc in next st, hdc in next st, (dc, tr, dc) in next st, rep from * around, end with (dc, tr) in same st as beg, sl st in top of beg ch-3 = 7 petals. Fasten off.

Rnd 5: Working in rnd-4 bk lps only, join C bet any 2 petals, ch 3 for first dc, * hdc in next st, sc in next st, hdc in next st, (dc, tr, dc) in next st bet rnd-4 petals, rep from * around, end with (dc, tr) in same st as beg, sl st in top of beg ch-3. Fasten off.

Large flower: Make 1 large flower working colors as foll: use purple for A, medium lavender for B, and medium blue for C.

Rnds 1-4: With size #6 hook and 3 strands of floss, work as for small flower rnds 1-4.

Rnd 5: Working in rnd-4 bk lps only, join C bet any 2 petals, ch 3 for first dc, hdc in same st, * hdc in next st, sc in next st, hdc in next st, (hdc, dc, tr, dc, hdc) in next st bet rnd-4 petals, rep from * around, end with (hdc, dc, tr) in same st as beg, sl st in top of beg ch-3. Fasten off.

Front base ring: With 3 strands of hand-dyed floss and size #7 hook, ch 100, join with a sl st to form a ring.

Rnd 1: Ch 1, sc in ea ch around, sl st in beg ch-1. Fasten off.

Joining flowers: With size #7 hook, join hand-dyed floss with sl st in tip of any petal on large flower, ch 4, drop lp from hook, insert hook in tip of any petal on first small flower and join to large flower with sl st, ch 3, sl st in next petal on small flower, ch 3, sl st in any petal on 2nd small flower, ch 3, sl st in next petal on same small flower, ch 4, sk next petal on large flower, sl st in next petal, ch 4, sl st in next petal on 2nd small flower, ch 9, sl st in any sc on base ring, ch 11, sk next petal on 2nd small flower, sl st in next petal, ch 18, sk 16 sc on base ring, sl st in next sc, ch 8, sl st in 8th ch on prev ch-18, ch 11, sk 2 petals on first small flower, sl st in next petal, ch 9, sk 16 sc on base ring, sl st in next sc, ch 9, sk next petal on first small flower, sl st in next petal, ch 6, sl st in same place on large flower as beg, ch 13, sk 10 sc on base ring, sl st in next sc, ch 11, sl st in next petal on large flower, ch 10, sk 13 sc on base ring, sl st in next sc, ch 10, sl st in next petal on large flower, ch 11, sk 8 sc on base ring, sl st in next sc, ch 11, sl st in next petal on large flower, ch 10, sk 8 sc on base ring, sl st in next sc, ch 10, sl st in next petal on large flower, ch 11, sk 13 sc on base ring, sl st in next sc, ch 13, sl st in next petal on large flower. Fasten off.

Back base ring: With 3 strands of hand-dyed floss and size #7 hook, ch 100, join with a sl st to form a ring.

Rnd 1: Ch 1, sc in ea ch around, sl st in beg ch-1. Fasten off.

Joining ring: With hand-dyed floss and size #7 hook, ch 32, join with a sl st to form a ring.

Ch 18, sl st in any sc on base ring, sl st in ea ch of ch-18, sc in ea of next 4 sts on joining ring, ch 18, sk 9 sc on base ring, sl st in next sc, sl st in ea ch of ch-18, sc in ea of next 4 sts on joining ring, ch 30, sk 9 sc on base ring, sl st in next sc, sl st in ea ch of ch-30, sc in ea of next 4 sts on joining ring, ch 30, sk 19 sc on base ring, sl st in next sc, sl st in ea ch of ch-30, sc in ea of next 4 sts on joining ring, ch 18, sk 9 sc on base ring, sl st in next sc, sl st in ea ch of ch-18, sc in ea of next 4 sts on joining ring, ch 18, sk 9 sc on base ring, sl st in next sc, sl st in ea ch of ch-18, sc in ea of next 4 sts on joining ring, ch 25, sk 9 sc on base ring, sl st in next sc, sl st in ea ch of ch-25, sc in ea of next 4 sts on joining ring, ch 25, sk 19 sc on base ring, sl st in next sc, sl st in ea ch of ch-25, sc in last 4 sts on joining ring, join with a sl st in first ch on beg ch-18. Fasten off.

Finishing: Dip egg halves in gloss and mold over plastic egg to shape. Let dry.

Beginning at top of ornament and leaving a 7" tail, buttonhole-stitch egg halves together with purple ribbon. Cut ribbon, leaving a 7" tail. Knot tails together at top of egg and knot ends together for hanger.

Cut 1 (13") piece and 1 (19") piece of purple ribbon. Knot purple and jade ribbons at top of egg. Tie a bow in jade ribbon and knot each end. Tie knots about 3" apart in purple ribbon streamers. Tack seed beads to jade ribbon as desired. Tack bugle beads to purple ribbon as desired.

Butterfly Ornament

Materials

Embroidery floss (8-yd. skein): 2 ecru; 1 each dark purple, medium purple, light purple, wine, medium pink, light pink.

Acrylic paints: light pink, light purple, medium purple, dark purple.

Paintbrush.

Sizes #7 and #9 steel crochet hooks.

Finish coat gloss.
Plastic egg pantyhose container.
3 yards (1/16"-wide) purple satin ribbon.
Small bunch of dried flowers.
Clear glue.

Directions

To dye ecru floss, see note under flower ornament.

Egg half (make 2): With size #7 hook and 3 strands of hand-dyed floss, ch 50, join with a sl st to form a ring.

Rnd 1: Ch 1, sc in ea st around, sl st in beg ch-1 = 50 sts.

Rnd 2: (Ch 5, sk 1 sc, sc in next sc) around, end with ch 5, sl st in base of beg ch-5.

Rnd 3: Sl st into center of lp, (ch 6, sc in next lp) around, sl st in base of beg ch-6.

Rnds 4-6: Rep rnd 3.

Rnd 7: Sl st into center of next lp, (ch 3, sc in next lp) around, sl st in base of beg ch-3.

Rnd 8: Ch 2 for first hdc, hdc in ea ch and sc around, sl st in top of beg ch-2. Fasten off.

Butterfly: Make 2 butterflies working colors as specified. Use 3 strands of floss. For first butterfly, use dark purple for A, light purple for B, and medium purple for C. For 2nd butterfly, use wine for A, light pink for B, and medium pink for C. Leave a 3" tail of thread at beg of ea butterfly.

With size #9 hook and A, ch 8, sc in 2nd ch from hook and ea of next 5 ch, 3 sc in last ch, working back along opposite side of ch, sc in ea of next 6 ch.

Rnd 1: Sl st in first sc, ch 12, sk next sc, sl st in next sc, ch 10, sk 3 sc, sl st in next sc, 3 sc in next st (tail), sl st in next st, ch 10, sk 3 sc, sl st in next sc, ch 12, sk next sc, sl st in next sc, sc in next st (head), sl st in first ch of beg ch-10. Do not fasten off.

Rnd 2: Join B with sl st in same st, carry A across by working over it, with B work 14 hdc in ch-12 lp, sl st in sl st bet lps, join C and carry A and B across, 12 hdc in ch-10 lp, pick up A and carry B and C across, sc in ea of next 3 sts, sl st in first ch of ch-10 lp, pick up C and carry A and B across, 12 hdc in ch-10 lp, sl st in sl st bet lps, pick up B and carry A and C across, 14 hdc in

ch-12 lp, pick up A and carry B and C across, sc in next st, hdc in next st, sc in next st (head), sl st in beg ch-1. Fasten off all threads, leaving a 3" tail of A. Pull both 3" tails of thread up through top of head for antenna. Tie a knot in each thread 1" from body. Cut thread close to knot.

Finishing: Dip butterflies in gloss; set aside. Dip egg halves in gloss and mold over plastic egg to shape. Let dry.

Beginning at top of ornament and leaving a 12" tail, whipstitch egg halves together with ribbon, working around base ring of each piece and stitching through each loop. Cut ribbon, leaving a 12" tail. Knot and tie tails of ribbon in a bow at top of egg. For hanger, cut a 6" length of ribbon, thread through top of ornament, and knot ends. Whipstitch butterflies to edge of circle with matching floss (see photo). Glue dried flowers around edge of circle, as desired.

Daffodil Ornament

Materials

Embroidery floss (8-yd. skein): 2 ecru; 1 each yellow, green.

Acrylic paints: yellow, light green, medium green.

Paintbrush.

Size #7 steel crochet hook.

Finish coat gloss.

Plastic egg pantyhose container.

32" (1/8"-wide) green satin ribbon.

25" (1/16"-wide) light green satin ribbon.

25" (1/16"-wide) yellow satin ribbon.

Directions

To dye ecru floss, see note under flower ornament.

Front: With 3 strands of hand-dyed floss, ch 96, join with a sl st to form a ring.

Rnd 1: Ch 2 for first hdc, hdc in ea ch around, sl st in top of beg ch-2.

Rnd 2: (Ch 8, sk 5 sts, sc in next st) around, end with ch 8, sl st in first ch of beg ch-8.

double-leaf flowers and join to leaf with sl st, ch 15, sl st in 6th ch from hook to form center ring of flower. Fasten off.

Make petals as for double-leaf flower. Fasten off.

Make another single-leaf flower in ch-4 lp on opposite side of egg.

Joining: Rnd 1: Join hand-dyed floss with a sl st in center petal of any flower, (ch 4, drop lp from hook, insert hook in center petal of next flower and join to first flower with sl st) 3 times, ch 4, sl st in beg sl st.

Rnd 2: Ch 1, * sc in ea of next 2 sts, ch 15, sl st in ch-4 lp on egg bet flowers, working back up ch-15, sl st in ea of next 6 ch, ch 7, sl st in next ch from hook, sc in next ch, hdc in next ch, dc in next ch, hdc in next ch, sc in next ch, (leaf made), sl st in ea of rem 8 ch on ch-15, sc in ea of next 2 ch on joining ring, sc in sl st of petal, rep from * 3 times more, end with sl st in beg ch-1. Fasten off.

Back: Work as for front rnds 1-3.

Joining: With hand-dyed floss, ch 20, join with a sl st to form a ring.

Rnd 1: (Ch 15, join to base ring and make a leaf as in rnd 2 of joining above, sc in ea of next 5 ch on ch-20 ring, sk 1 ch-4 lp on base ring) 4 times, sl st in first ch of beg ch-15. Fasten off.

Finishing: Dip egg halves in gloss and mold over plastic egg to shape. Let dry.

Whipstitch egg halves together with 1 strand of green floss. For hanger, cut a 7" length of ⅛"-wide green ribbon, thread through top of ornament and knot ends. Tie remaining ribbons together in a bow at top of ornament. Tie knots about 3" apart in each ribbon streamer.

Rnd 3: Ch 7 for first dc and ch 4, dc in same st, * ch 5, sc in next sc, ch 5, (dc, ch 4, dc) in next sc, rep from * around, end with sl st in 3rd ch of beg ch-7. Fasten off.

Double-leaf flower: With green, * ch 10, sl st in 2nd ch from hook, sc in next st, hdc in ea of next 2 sts, dc in ea of next 2 sts, hdc in ea of next 2 sts, sc in last st (leaf made), rep from * once more for 2nd leaf, drop lp from hook, insert hook in any ch-4 lp on egg and join to leaf with a sl st, ch 15, sl st in 6th ch from hook to form center ring of flower. Fasten off.

Petals: Join yellow with sl st in ring, * ch 6, draw up a lp in 2nd ch from hook and ea rem ch, yo and through all lps (petal made), rep from * 4 times more, end with sl st in base of first petal. Fasten off.

Sk 3 ch-4 lps on egg and make another double-leaf flower in next ch-4 lp.

Single-leaf flower: With green, ch 10 and make 1 leaf as for double-leaf flower above, drop lp from hook, insert hook in center ch-4 lp bet

Holiday Trimmings

Christmas Tree

Finished Size

Approximately 13" tall.

Materials

Size 5 pearl cotton (218-yd. ball): 3 emerald.
Size #7 steel crochet hook, or size to obtain gauge.
13"-high craft foam cone with 4"-diameter base.
½ yard of green cotton fabric.
Green sewing thread.
Straight pins.
Miniature ornaments.

Gauge

Scallop = 2½".

Directions

Row 1: Ch 12, dc in 6th ch from hook, (ch 1, sk 1 st, dc in next st) 3 times = 4 sps, ch 4, turn.

Rows 2-4: Dc in next dc, (ch 1, dc in next dc) twice, ch 1, dc in 3rd ch of tch, ch 4, turn. Do not ch 4 at the end of row 4.

Turn and work scallop down side edge of mesh as foll: ch 5, sk 1 sp, 3 dc in next sp, ch 5, 3 dc in next sp, ch 2, sk 2 ch, dc in next ch, ch 5, turn, sc in next sp, ch 5, sc in center dc of next dc-grp, ch 5, (3 dc, ch 5, 3 dc) in next sp, ch 5, sc in center dc of next dc-grp, ch 5, sc in next sp, ch 5, sk 2 ch, sc in next ch of same sp, turn, (ch 6, sc in next lp, ch 6, sc in same lp) 3 times, ch 6, sc in center dc of next dc-grp, ch 6, sc in next lp, (ch 6, sc in same lp) 3 times, ch 6, sc in center dc of next dc-grp, (ch 6, sc in next lp, ch 6, sc in same

lp) 3 times, turn, * (ch 3, sc) twice in next lp, rep from * 17 times more, ch 3, sc in top of first dc of mesh.

Row 5: Work across mesh as foll: ch 4, dc in next dc, (ch 1, dc in next dc) twice, ch 1, sk 1 ch, dc in 3rd ch of tch, ch 4, turn.

Rep rows 2-5 until piece measures 86", or desired length to cover cone.

Finishing: Use ½" seam. From green fabric, cut 1 (12" x 14") rectangle and 1 (4"-diameter) circle. Wrap fabric rectangle around cone. Trim to fit, adding ½" seam allowance. Turn under seam allowance along sides and slipstitch together, forming a point at top of cone. Turn under seam allowance around 4" circle and around fabric at base of cone. Slipstitch circle to fabric cone to cover bottom of foam cone.

Starting at bottom of cone and with scallops pointing down, wrap crochet tightly around cone in a spiral, pinning to secure. Decorate tree with ornaments as desired.

Greeting Cards

Finished Size

Each sweater is approximately 4½" x 2¼".

Materials (for 3 cards)

Peach and green sweater: scraps of peach sportweight acrylic-mohair blend; scraps of green sportweight acrylic.
Gray sweater: scraps of gray worsted-weight wool.
Ivory sweater: scraps of ivory worsted-weight acrylic; scraps of variegated sportweight cotton-blend bouclé.
Size #1 steel crochet hook.
3 small decorative crochet hooks (optional).
3 (6¼" x 4½") blank greeting cards.
Fabric glue.

Directions

Peach and green sweater: Row 1: With green, ch 10, sc in 2nd ch from hook and ea ch across = 9 sts, turn. Fasten off.

Row 2: Join peach, ch 1, (sk 1 st, sc in next st, sk 1 st, 2 sc in next st) twice, sk 1 st, sc in last st, turn. Fasten off.

Row 3: Join green, (ch 3, sk 1 st, sc in next st) 5 times, turn.

Row 4: (Ch 3, sc in next lp) 5 times, turn. Fasten off.

Row 5: Join peach in first ch-3 lp, ch 3 for first dc, dc in same lp, (3 dc in next lp) 3 times, 2 dc in last lp. Do not turn. Fasten off.

Row 6: With right side of row 5 facing, join green in top of beg ch-3, ch 5. Fasten off. Join green at other end of row 5, ch 6, turn, sc in 2nd ch from hook and ea of 4 ch, sc in ea st across body of sweater and ea of 5 ch, turn.

Rows 7 and 8: (Ch 3, sk 1 st, sc in next st) across, turn. Fasten off after row 8.

Row 9: Join peach with sc in first lp, (ch 2, sc in next lp) 3 times. Drop last lp from hook. Do not work rem sts or fasten off. Leaving a tail 1 yard long, cut yarn.

Gray sweater: Cut a 12" piece of yarn and set aside.

Row 1: Ch 10, sc in 2nd ch from hook and ea ch across = 9 sts, turn.

Row 2: Ch 2 for first hdc, hdc in next st, [sk 1 st, 2 hdc in next st (shell made)] twice, sk 1 st, hdc in ea of next 2 sts, turn.

Rows 3 and 4: Ch 2 for first hdc, hdc in next st, (2 hdc bet shells) 3 times, hdc in ea of last 2 sts, ch 6, turn. Drop lp from hook. Do not fasten off.

Row 5: Join 12" piece of yarn at other end of row 4, ch 5. Fasten off. Pick up lp at other end of row, sc in 2nd ch from hook and ea rem ch, sc in ea st across body of sweater and ea of 5 ch, turn.

Row 6: Ch 1, sc in ea st across, turn.

Row 7: Ch 1, sc in ea of next 6 sts. Fasten off. Sk 3 sts, join yarn in next st, ch 1, sc in ea rem st. Drop last lp from hook. Do not fasten off. Leaving a tail 1 yard long, cut yarn.

Ivory sweater: Cut a 12" piece of variegated bouclé and set aside.

Row 1: With ivory, ch 10, sc in 2nd ch from hook and ea ch across = 9 sts, turn.

Rows 2-4: Working in bk lps only, ch 1, sc in ea st across, turn.

Row 5: Ch 1, sc in ea of next 3 sts, join variegated bouclé, cut ivory, sc in ea rem st across, ch 6, turn. Drop lp from hook. Do not fasten off.

Row 6: Join 12" piece of variegated bouclé at other end of row 5, ch 5. Fasten off. Pick up lp at other end of row, sc in 2nd ch from hook and ea rem ch, sc in ea of next 4 sc, insert hook in st 2 rows below next st, draw up a long lp and complete st as sc (sc spike st made), sc spike st in next st, sc in ea of rem 4 sc and ea of 5 ch, turn.

Row 7: Ch 1, sc in ea of next 6 sts, cut variegated bouclé, join ivory, working in bk lps only, sc in ea st across, turn.

Row 8: Ch 1, working in bk lps only, sc in ea st across, turn.

Row 9: Ch 1, sc in ea of next 12 sts, cut ivory, join variegated bouclé, sc in ea of next 4 sts. Drop last lp from hook. Do not work rem sts or fasten off. Leaving a tail 1 yard long, cut yarn.

Loops: Join variegated bouclé in center of body of sweater, (ch 6, sc in next st) twice, fasten off.

Finishing: For each card, wind tail of yarn into a small ball. If desired, insert decorative crochet hook into loop of last stitch. Arrange sweater, ball of yarn, and hook on greeting card and glue in place.

Jack-o'-lanterns

Finished Size

Approximately 35" x 46".

Materials

Sportweight wool (124-yd. ball): 8 dark rust, 5 medium rust, 4 coral.

Worsted-weight wool-blend (150-yd. skein): 2 dark green, 1 green.

Size E crochet hook, or size to obtain gauge.

Gauge

4 hdc and 3 rows = 1".

Directions

Octagon (make 9 dark rust, 6 medium rust, 5 coral): Ch 4, join with a sl st to form a ring.

Rnd 1: Ch 1, 15 sc in ring, sl st in beg ch-1.

Rnd 2: Ch 2 for first hdc, hdc in same st, (hdc in next st, 2 hdc in next st) 7 times, hdc in last st, sl st in top of beg ch = 24 sts.

Rnd 3: Ch 2 for first hdc, sk next st, * 2 hdc bet next 2 sts for corner, (hdc bet next 2 sts), rep from * 6 times more, hdc bet next 2 sts, sl st in top of beg ch = 32 sts.

Rnd 4: Sl st in next st, sl st bet next 2 hdc, ch 2 for first hdc, * (hdc bet next 2 sts) 3 times, 2 hdc in next st for corner, rep from * around, end with hdc in same sp as beg ch-2, sl st in top of beg ch = 40 sts.

Rnd 5: Ch 2 for first hdc, * (hdc bet next 2 sts) 4 times, 2 hdc bet next 2 sts for corner, rep from * around, end with hdc in same sp as beg ch-2, sl st in top of beg ch = 48 sts.

Rnds 6-14: Work around octagon as est in rnd 5, inc 1 st bet corners ea rnd = 120 sts after rnd 14.

Rnd 15: Ch 2 for first hdc, * (hdc bet next 2 sts) 14 times, (hdc, ch 1, hdc) bet next 2 sts for corner, rep from * around, end with hdc in same

sp as beg ch-2, ch 1, sl st in top of beg ch-2 = 128 sts. Fasten off.

Edging: Join dark rust in any corner and work around ea octagon in crab st (reverse sc) as foll: with right side facing and working from left to right, sc in corner st, (ch 1, sc in next st) around. Fasten off.

Embroidery: Referring to photo and diagram, use 1 strand of dark green to embroider a surface ch-st jack-o'-lantern on ea of 5 coral octagons.

To work surface ch-st, make a sl knot in yarn. With right side of octagon facing, insert hook through fabric bet 2 sts and draw up a lp. Insert hook bet next 2 sts, draw up a lp and draw through lp on hook. Cont working surface ch-sts to embroider eyes, nose, and mouth according to diagram. Work in rows to completely fill ea design area with surface ch-sts.

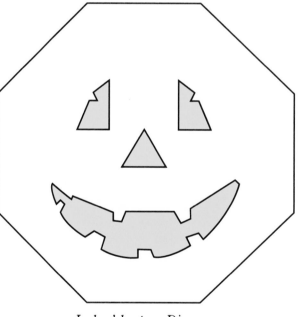

Jack-o'-lantern Diagram

Block (make 12): **Row 1:** With dark green, ch 16 loosely, hdc in 3rd ch from hook and ea ch across, pulling first lp of ea st up ½" = 15 sts, turn.

Rows 2-8: Ch 2 for first hdc, working in ft lps only, hdc loosely in ea st across, turn.

Edging: (Ch 1, 2 sc in side of ea row to corner, ch 1, sc in ea st to corner) twice, ch 1, sl st in beg ch-1. Fasten off, leaving a tail of yarn.

Assembly: Arrange octagons as desired for a throw 4 motifs wide and 5 motifs long. With wrong sides facing and using dark rust yarn, whipstitch octagons together through back loops only. Using tail of yarn and working in back loops only, whipstitch a dark green block in the center of each group of 4 octagons.

3-leaf spray (make 3 dark green, 1 light green): **First leaf:** Ch 16. **Row 1:** Work 6 tr in 5th ch from hook, turn.

Row 2: Ch 3 for first dc, [keeping last lp of ea st on hook, dc in ea of next 2 tr, yo and through all lps on hook (dc dec made)] twice, dc in next tr, turn.

Row 3: Ch 2 for first hdc, dc dec over next 2 sts, hdc in top of tch, turn.

Row 4: Ch 1 for first sc, sc in top of next st, turn.

Row 5: Ch 3, sl st in sc for tip of leaf, working down side of leaf in ends of rows, ch 2, sl st in next row, ch 3, sl st in next row, ch 4, sl st in base of leaf.

2nd leaf: Ch 9, rep rows 1-5 of first leaf, sc in ea of 4 ch on ch-9.

3rd leaf: Ch 5, rep rows 1-5 of first leaf, sc in ea of 11 ch on beg ch-16. Fasten off.

6-leaf spray (make 2): With light green, work as for first and 2nd leaves of 3-leaf spray. Ch 16 and work another 3-leaf spray as est, do not sc in ea of 11 ch after 3rd leaf. Sc in ea of next 7 ch on ch-16, ch 5, rep rows 1-5 of first leaf, sc in ea of next 4 ch on ch-16, sc in base of leaf, sc in ea of 4 ch, sc in base of leaf, sc in ea of 11 ch on beg ch-16. Fasten off.

Vine (make 3 dark green, 2 light green): Ch 76, sc in 2nd ch from hook and ea ch across. Fasten off.

Finishing: Arrange leaf sprays and vines on afghan as desired and tack to secure (see photo).

Poinsettia Throw

Poinsettia Throw

Finished Size

Approximately 36" x 42".

Materials

Bulky-weight wool (105-yd. skein): 14 forest green.

Sizes E, F, and H crochet hooks, or size to obtain gauge.

Sportweight wool (124-yd. ball) 1 red.

4 gold buttons.

Gauge

13 dc and 8 rows = 4" with size H hook.

Directions

Side panel (make 2): **Row 1:** With forest green and size H hook, ch 50, dc in 4th ch from hook and ea ch across, turn = 48 sts.

Row 2: Ch 3 for first dc, * yo twice, insert hook from front to back around post of next st, complete st as a tr (tr/rf made), dc in next st, sk 3 sts, dtr in ea of next 3 sts, working behind prev 3-dtr, dtr in ea of 3 sk sts (cable made), dc in next st, tr/rf around post of next st, dc in next st **, sk 3 sts, dtr in ea of next 3 sts, working in front of prev 3-dtr, dtr in ea of 3 sk sts, dc in next st, rep from * twice more, end last rep at **, turn.

Row 3: Ch 3 for first dc, * yo twice, insert hook from back to front around post of next tr, complete st as a tr (tr/rb made), dc in next dc, sk 3 dtr, dtr in ea of next 3 dtr, working in front of prev 3-dtr, dtr in ea of 3 sk dtr, dc in next dc, tr/rb around post of next tr, dc in next dc **, sk 3 dtr, dtr in ea of next 3 dtr, working behind prev 3-dtr, dtr in ea of 3 sk dtr, dc in next dc, rep from * twice more, end last rep at **, turn.

Row 4: Ch 3 for first dc, * tr/rf around post of next tr, dc in next dc, sk 3 dtr, dtr in ea of next 3 dtr, working behind prev 3-dtr, dtr in ea of 3 sk dtr, dc in next dc, tr/rf around post of next tr **, dc in ea of next 26 sts, rep from * to ** once, dc in last st, turn.

Row 5: Ch 3 for first dc, * tr/rb around post of next tr, dc in next dc, sk 3 dtr, dtr in ea of next 3 dtr, working in front of prev 3-dtr, dtr in ea of 3 sk dtr, dc in next dc, tr/rb around post of next tr **, dc in ea of next 26 dc, rep from * to ** once, dc in last st, turn.

Rows 6-19: Rep rows 4 and 5 alternately.

Rows 20-73: (Rep rows 2-19) 3 times.

Rows 74 and 75: Rep rows 2 and 3.

Row 76: Ch 3 for first dc, dc in ea st across. Fasten off.

Center panel (make 1): **Row 1:** With forest green and size H hook, ch 28, dc in 4th ch from hook and ea ch across, turn = 26 dc.

Row 2: Ch 3 for first dc, * sk 3 sts, dtr in ea of next 3 sts, working in front of prev 3-dtr, dtr in ea of 3 sk sts, dc in next st **, tr/rf around post of next st, dc in next st, sk 3 sts, dtr in ea of next 3 sts, working behind prev 3-dtr, dtr in ea of 3 sk sts, dc in next st, tr/rf around post of next st, dc in next st, rep from * to ** once, turn.

Row 3: Ch 3 for first dc, * sk 3 dtr, dtr in ea of next 3 dtr, working behind prev 3-dtr, dtr in ea of 3 sk dtr, dc in next dc **, tr/rb around post of next tr, dc in next dc, sk 3 dtr, dtr in ea of next 3 dtr, working in front of prev 3-dtr, dtr in ea of 3 sk dtr, dc in next dc, tr/rb around post of next tr, dc in next dc, rep from * to ** once, turn.

Rows 4-19: Ch 3 for first dc, dc in ea st across, turn = 26 dc.

Rows 20-73: (Rep rows 2-19) 3 times.

Rows 74 and 75: Rep rows 2 and 3.

Row 76: Ch 3 for first dc, dc in ea st across. Fasten off.

Assembly: With right sides up and cables aligned, whipstitch a side panel to ea long edge of center panel.

Poinsettia: Large petal (make 24): With size F hook and red, ch 18, sl st in 2nd ch from hook and ea of next 2 ch, sc in next ch, dc in next ch, tr in ea of next 3 ch, dtr in ea of next 5 ch, tr in next ch, dc in next ch, hdc in next ch, [sc, ch 5, sl st in 4th ch from hook to make a picot, ch 1, sc] in next ch (point of petal), working down opposite side of foundation ch, hdc in next ch, dc in next ch, tr in next ch, dtr in ea of next 5 ch, tr in ea of next 3 ch, dc in next ch, sc in next ch, sl st in ea of next 3 ch. Fasten off.

Medium petal (make 5): With size E hook, work as for large petal.

Small petal (make 15): With size E hook and red, ch 11, sl st in 2nd ch from hook and next ch,

sc in next ch, dc in next ch, tr in ea of next 3 ch, dc in next ch, hdc in next ch, [sc, ch 5, sl st in 4th ch from hook to make a picot, ch 1, sc] in next ch (point of petal), working down opposite side of foundation ch, hdc in next ch, dc in next ch, tr in ea of next 3 ch, dc in next ch, sc in next ch, sl st in ea of next 2 ch. Fasten off.

Finishing: Arrange petals on throw to form 4 poinsettias (see photo) and tack in place. Stitch a button in the center of each poinsettia.

133

Sparkling Ornaments

Icicles

Finished Size

A: Approximately 4½" long x 2" wide.
B: Approximately 5½" long x 1¾" wide.
C: Approximately 6" long x 2" wide.

Materials

Size 10 crochet cotton (400-yd. ball): 1 white.
Metallic thread (1000m spool): 1 each of 2 shades of silver.
Size #3 steel crochet hook.
13 (¼"-long) cone-shaped crystal beads.
Clear seed beads.
Beading needle.

Directions

Note: For crochet, use 1 strand each of crochet cotton and 2 metallic threads (3 threads held together as 1).

Use 2 strands of silver thread and beading needle to attach beads to ornaments. Use clear seed beads with crystal beads, as desired (see photo).

Icicle A: Top ring: Ch 6, join with a sl st to form a ring. Ch 2 for first hdc, 12 hdc in ring.

2nd ring: Row 1: Ch 6, join with a sl st in first ch to form another ring, turn.

Row 2: Ch 3 for first dc, 10 dc in ring, dc in same sl st as joining, turn.

Row 3: (Ch 3, sk 2 sts, sc in next st) 3 times, sk 2 sts, dc in next st, turn.

Row 4: (Ch 3, sc in next lp) twice, dc in next lp, turn.

Row 5: Ch 3, sc in next lp, dc in next lp, turn.

Row 6: Ch 3 for first dc, dc in same lp, ch 6, sl st in 4th ch from hook to make a picot, ch 3, 2 dc in next lp, turn.

Row 7: Loosely ch 6, sk picot lp, yo 4 times, insert hook in last dc on row 6, (yo and pull through 2 lps) 5 times (tr tr made), ch 8, sl st in top of tr tr, ch 10, sl st in same st, ch 8, sl st in same st. Fasten off.

Trim: Join threads in joining st of first ring, ch 1, (sc, ch 5, sc) in ea st around = 13 lps, sl st in beg ch. Fasten off.

Finishing: Referring to photo, stitch 1 crystal bead to each bottom loop, 1 crystal bead to row-6 picot, and 1 crystal bead to row-5 single crochet stitch.

Icicle B: Small ring: Ch 18, join with a sl st to form a ring. Ch 1, sc in ea of next 5 ch, (ch 3, sc in next ch) twice, ch 4, sc in next ch, ch 5, sc in next ch, ch 4, sc in next ch, (ch 3, sc in next ch) twice, sc in ea of next 5 ch, sl st in beg ch-1 = top of ring. Fasten off.

Center ring: Ch 26, join with a sl st to form a ring. Ch 1, sc in ea of next 8 ch, (ch 3, sc in next ch) twice, (ch 4, sc in next ch) twice, ch 5, sc in next ch, (ch 4, sc in next ch) twice, (ch 3, sc in next ch) twice, sc in ea of next 8 ch, sl st in beg ch-1 = top of ring. Fasten off, leaving a tail of white.

Bottom ring: Ch 36, join with a sl st to form a ring. Ch 1, sc in ea of next 10 ch, (ch 3, sc in next ch) twice, (ch 4, sc in next ch) 3 times, (ch 5, sc in next ch) twice, ch 7, sc in next ch, (ch 5, sc in next ch) twice, (ch 4, sc in next ch) 3 times, (ch 3, sc in next ch) twice, sc in ea of next 10 ch, sl st in beg ch-1 = top of ring. Fasten off, leaving a tail of white.

Assembly: Use tails of thread to stitch rings together. With small ring right side up, stitch top of center ring to bottom of small ring behind chain-5 loop (see photo). Stitch top of bottom ring to bottom of center ring behind chain-5 loop.

Finishing: Referring to photo, stitch 1 crystal bead inside top ring, 1 crystal bead each to chain-5 loop on top and center rings, and 1 crystal bead to chain-7 loop on bottom ring.

Icicle C: Large ring: Ch 51, join with a sl st to form a ring.

    Rnd 1: Ch 1, sc in ea of next 18 ch, 2 sc in next ch, sc in ea of next 13 ch, 2 sc in next ch, sc in ea of next 18 ch, sl st in beg ch-1.

    Rnd 2: Working in bk lps only, sl st in ea of next 7 sts, (ch 3, sl st in ea of next 3 sts) twice, ch 4, sl st in ea of next 4 sts, ch 4, sl st in ea of next 2 sts, (ch 4, sc in next st) 7 times, ch 11, sk 1 st, sc in next st, ch 1, turn, working in ch-11 lp, sc in ea of 11 ch, sl st in sc before ch-11 lp, ch 1, turn, sl st in ea of next 5 sts, (sl st, ch 5, sl st) in next st, sl st in ea of next 5 sts (bottom lp made), (ch 4, sc in next st) 7 times, ch 4, sl st in ea of next 2 sts, ch 4, sl st in ea of next 4 sts, (ch 3, sl st in ea of next 3 sts) twice, ch 3, sl st in ea of next 7 sts, ch 1, turn work to wrong side, sl st in beg sl st.

    Top ring: Ch 24, sl st in 18th ch from hook to form a ring, working around this ring, sl st in ea of next 7 ch, ch 3, sc in next ch, ch 4, sc in next ch, ch 5, sc in next ch, ch 4, sc in next ch, ch 3, sl st in ea of next 7 ch of ring, sl st in ea rem ch of beg ch-24 to large ring, ch 6 for small lp, sl st in first ch of ch-6 lp. Fasten off.

Finishing: Referring to photo, attach crystal beads as follows: stitch 1 bead inside top ring, 1 bead to small loop at top of large ring, 1 bead to skipped single crochet stitch on round-2, and 1 bead to loop at bottom of large ring.

Garland

Finished Size

Approximately 3¾ yards long.

Materials

    Metallic thread (1000m spool): 1 each of 2 shades of silver.

    105 (¼"-long) cone-shaped crystal beads.

    10 (¾") diamond-shaped crystal beads.

    10 (½") hexagon-shaped crystal beads.

    Size #10 steel crochet hook.

Directions

Twist 1 strand of each metallic thread together and string all the beads onto twisted threads before beginning to crochet. String beads in the following order: 5 cone beads, 1 diamond bead, 5 cone beads, 1 hexagon bead.

Row 1: * (Ch 8, pull up a cone bead) 5 times, ch 8, pull up a hexagon bead, (ch 8, pull up a cone bead) 5 times, ch 8, pull up a diamond bead, rep from * across until 5 cone beads rem, (ch 8, pull up a cone bead) 5 times, ch 8, turn.

    Row 2: Dc in ea of next 5 ch, * ch 5, sk bead, dc in ea of next 4 ch, ch 3, sl st in top of prev dc to make a picot, dc in ea of next 4 ch, rep from * across. Fasten off.

General Directions

Gauge

Before beginning a project, work a 4"-square gauge swatch using the recommended-size hook. Measure an inch or two inches (as given in the gauge note); count and compare the number of stitches in the swatch with the designer's gauge. If you have fewer stitches in your swatch, try a smaller hook; if you have more stitches, try a larger hook.

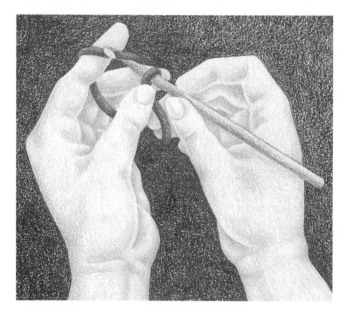

Working Together

Hold the hook as you would a pencil (shown here) or a piece of chalk. If your hook has a finger rest, position your thumb and opposing finger there for extra control. Weave the yarn through the fingers of your left hand to control the amount of yarn fed into the work and to provide tension. Once work has begun, the thumb and middle finger of the left hand come into play, pressing together to hold the stitches just made.

Crochet Abbreviations

beg	begin(ning)
bet	between
bk lp(s)	back loop(s)
ch	chain(s)
ch-	refers to chain previously made
cl	cluster(s)
cont	continu(e) (ing)
dc	double crochet
dec	decrease(s) (d) (ing)
dtr	double triple crochet
ea	each
est	established
foll	follow(s) (ing)
ft lp(s)	front loop(s)
grp(s)	group(s)
hdc	half double crochet
inc	increase(s) (d) (ing)
lp(s)	loop(s)
pat	pattern(s)
prev	previous
qdtr	quadruple triple crochet
rem	remain(s) (ing)
rep	repeat(s)
rnd(s)	round(s)
sc	single crochet
sk	skip
sl st	slip stitch
sp(s)	space(s)
st(s)	stitch(es)
tch	turning chain
tog	together
tr	triple crochet
tr tr	triple triple crochet
yo	yarn over

Repeat whatever follows * as indicated. "Rep from * 3 times more" means to work 4 times in all.

Work directions given in parentheses and brackets the number of times specified or in the place specified.

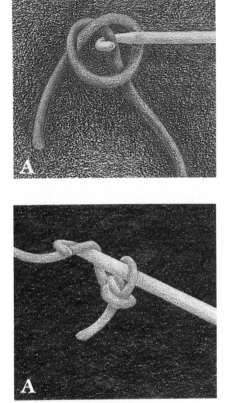

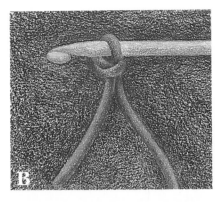

Slip Knot Diagram

Loop the yarn around and let the loose end of the yarn fall behind the loop to form a pretzel shape as shown. Insert the hook (**A**) and pull both ends to close the knot (**B**).

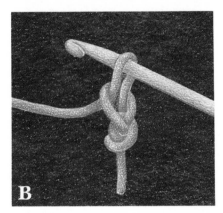

Chain Stitch Diagram

A. Place a slip knot on your hook. With hands in the position shown above, wrap the yarn up and over the hook (from back to front). This movement is called a "yarn over (yo)" and is basic to every crochet stitch.

B. Use the hook to pull the yarn through the loop (lp) already on the hook. The combination of yo and pulling the yarn through the lp makes 1 chain stitch (ch.)

C. Repeat until the ch is the desired length, trying to keep the movements even and all the ch stitches (sts) the same size. Hold the ch near the working area to keep it from twisting. Count sts as shown in diagram.

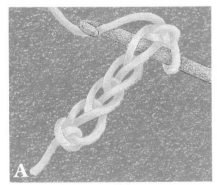

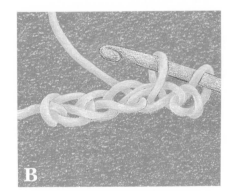

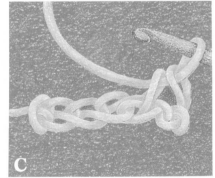

Single Crochet Diagram

A. Insert hook under top 2 lps of 2nd ch from hook and yo. (Always work sts through top 2 lps of each st unless instructions specify otherwise.)

B. Yo and pull yarn through ch (2 lps on hook).

C. Yo and pull yarn through 2 lps on hook (1 sc made).

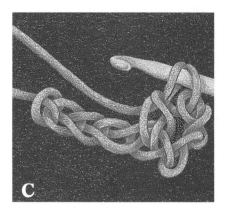

Double Crochet Diagram

A. Yo, insert hook into 4th ch from hook, and yo.

B. Pull yarn through ch (3 lps on hook).

C. Yo and pull through 2 lps on hook (2 lps remaining). (*Note:* When instructions say "keeping last lp of ea st on hook," this means to work the specified st to the final yo. This is done to make a cluster or to work a decrease.)

D. Yo and pull through 2 remaining (rem) lps (1 dc made).

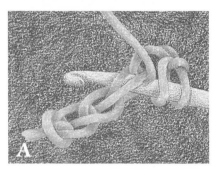

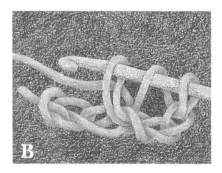

Half Double Crochet Diagram

A. Yo and insert hook into 3rd ch from hook.

B. Yo and pull through ch (3 lps on hook).

C. Yo and pull yarn through all 3 lps on hook (1 hdc made).

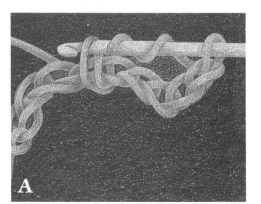

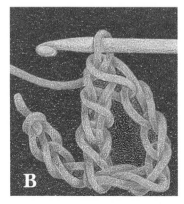

Triple Crochet Diagram

A. Yo twice, insert hook into 5th ch from hook. Yo and pull through ch (4 lps on hook).

B. Yo and pull through 2 lps on hook (3 lps rem). Yo and pull through 2 lps on hook (2 lps rem). Yo and pull through 2 lps on hook (1 tr made).

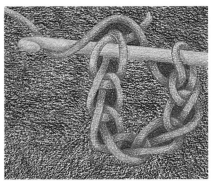

Slip Stitch Diagram

Here a slip stitch (sl st) is used to join a ring. Taking care not to twist ch, insert hook into first ch, yo and pull through ch and lp on hook (sl st made). The sl st can also be used to join finished squares or to move across a group of sts without adding height to the work.

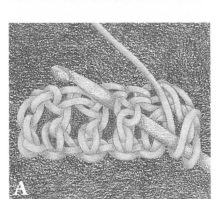

Working Around the Post

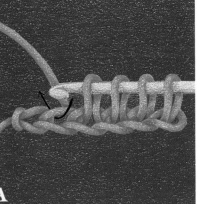

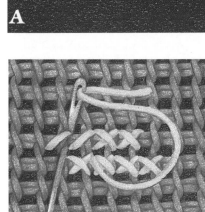

Afghan Stitch

A. *Row 1: Step 1:* Keeping all lps on hook, pull up a lp through top lp only, in 2nd ch from hook and each ch across = same number of lps and ch. Do not turn.
B. *Step 2:* Yo and pull through first lp on hook, * yo and pull through 2 lps on hook, rep from * across (1 lp rem on hook for first lp of next row). Do not turn.
C. *Row 2: Step 1:* Keeping all lps

on hook, pull up a lp from under 2nd vertical bar, * pull up a lp from under next vertical bar, rep from * across. Do not turn.
    Step 2: Rep step 2 of row 1.
    Rep both steps of row 2 for the required number of rows. Fasten off after last row by working a sl st in each bar across.
D. When the fabric is finished, it is a perfect grid for cross-stitch.

Yarn Information

The following is a complete list of the yarns used for each project pictured in the book. Visit your local yarn shop to obtain the yarn shown or for help in substituting another yarn. If you are unable to locate the yarn in your area or for further information, write the yarn company at the address listed below.

TOWN & COUNTRY

Blue Blanket, page 8, Aarlan, Cotonella (50-gr., 115-yd. ball): 15 Blue #6131, 4 White #6151.

Jewel Tones, page 10, Aarlan, Charmeuse (50-gr., 185-yd. skein): 7 Turquoise #4955, 1 Forest Green #4959, 5 Heather Peacock Blue #4977, 1 Dark Purple #4975, 3 Dark Blue #4975, 1 Medium Blue #4974, 3 Fuchsia #4970, 1 Green #4976, 1 Magenta #4971.

Grapevine, page 13, Pingouin, Le Yarn #3 (100-gr., 200-yd. skein): 15 Tan #406. Brunswick Yarns, Windrush (100-gr., 230-yd. skein): 1 each Jade Heather #9067, Blackberry Heather #90491, Dark Imari Rose #9058, Mauve-Lilac Heather #9088, Damask Rose Heather #90454, Pastel Heather #90496.

Midnight Rose, page 16, Brunswick Yarns, Pearl (50-gr., 110-yd. ball): 32 Black #5909.

Woven Rings, page 20, Brunswick Yarns, Pearl (50-gr., 110-yd. ball): 20 Silver Gray #5915, 19 Dusty Blue #5921, 15 Willow #5920 for afghan; 1 each Silver Gray #5915, Dusty Blue #5921, Willow #5920 for pillow.

For Baby, page 25, Pingouin, Douceur (50-gr., 75-yd. skein): 25 White.

Checkerboard, page 28, Classic Elite Yarns, Acadia (50-gr., 115-yd. skein): 19 Natural #2116. Tahki Imports, Designer Homespun Tweed (110-gr., 175-yd. skein): 5 Blue #203.

Soft Pastel Shells, page 30, Hayfield Yarns, Pretty Pastel 3-Ply (40-gr., 170-yd. skein): 6 each Green #009051, Pink #009053, Blue #009052, Yellow #009055, Lavender #064009 for throw; 2 each Green #009051, Pink #009053, Blue #009052, Yellow #009055, Lavender #064009 for robe.

Mohair Roses, page 34, Classic Elite Yarns, Applause (50-gr., 70-yd. skein): 11 each Apricot #6566, Eggshell #6516; La Gran (1.5-oz., 90-yd. skein): 9 Variegated Pastel #1801.

Black and White, page 37, Berroco, Cambridge Tweed (50-gr., 103-yd. ball): 17 White #9133. Brunswick Yarns, Pearl (50-gr., 110-yd. ball): 16 Black #5909. Pingouin, Oued (50-gr. 240-yd. ball): 2 White #15. Brunswick Yarns, Alaska (40-gr., 130-yd. ball): 3 Black #9204.

Artist's Palette, page 40, Lane Borgosesia, Tropical (50-gr., 170-yd. ball): 34 Variegated Pink/Yellow/Blue/Green #4.

HEARTH & HOME

Shades of Violet, page 44, Rowan Designer Collection, Cabled Mercerized Cotton (50-gr., 184-yd. ball): 9 each Mauve #311, Rich Purple #310; 2 Lichen #327.

Bolster Pillow, page 46, Bucilla, Wondersheen (400-yd. ball): 4 Aqua #25.

Have a Seat, page 49, Trendsetter Yarns, Bacio (50-gr., 76-yd. ball): 5 Black with Multicolor Slubs #15.

Bath Set, page 52, Schewe, Filigrana (50-gr., 137-yd. ball): 7 Aqua #4186; DMC Corporation, Perle Cotton, Size 3 (16-yd. skein): 6 Sky Blue-vy. lt. #747 (A), 11 Turquoise-lt. #598 (B). DMC Corporation, Perle Cotton, Size 5 (27-yd. skein): 4 Sky Blue-vy. lt. #747 (A), 2 Turquoise-lt. #598 (B) for bath towel edging; 1 each Terra Cotta-lt. #758 (A), Peach-lt. #754 (B), Peach Pecan-lt. #951 (C) for hand towel edging; 1 each Sky Blue-vy. lt. #747 (A), Turquoise-lt. #598 (B) for washcloth edging.

Red Rose Doily, page 55, Coats & Clark, Size 30: 1 (250-yd. ball) each Shaded Pinks #15, Shaded Greens #21; 2 (350-yd. balls) White.

Slip Into Satin, page 58, DMC Corporation, Perle Cotton, Size 8 (95-yd. ball): 10 Black #310.

Dinnertime, page 62, Kreinik Mfg. Co. Inc., Tandoori Tussah 1-ply (400-gr. cone): 1 Ecru.

Pansies Galore, page 64, Aarlan, Cotonella (50-gr., 115-yd. ball): 8 Blue #6146. DMC Corporation, Perle Cotton, Size 3 (16-yd. skein): 2 each White, Yellow #744, Light Pink #818, Light Salmon #353, Lavender #554, Purple #552, Black #310, Green #701; 1 each Pale Yellow #745, Pink #894, Rose #962, Salmon #352, Dark Salmon #351, Light Brick #3328, Brick #221, Burgundy #816, Medium Green #909, Dark Green #911.

Pins 'n Needles, page 68, DMC Corporation, Cebelia, Size 30 (563-yd. ball): 1 Peach #754. DMC Corporation, Cebelia, Size 20 (405-yd. ball): 1 Ecru #3033.

Mantel Elegance, page 71, Coats & Clark, Size 30 (150-yd. ball): 9 Ecru.

GIFTS & FRILLS

Pretty Pink Basket, page 76, Aarlan, Fleurette (50-gr., 120-yd. ball): 4 Pink #C4473.

Three Pairs of Mittens, page 81, Gray: Filatura Di Crosa, Sympathie (50-gr., 150-yd. skein): 1 Gray #932. Brunswick Yarns, Pearl (50-gr., 110-yd. ball): 1 Plum #5926. Green and Red: Filatura Di Crosa, Sympathie (50-gr., 150-yd. skein): 2 Forest Green #938. Aarlan, Swa Laine (50-gr., 105-yd. skein): 1 Dark Red #R2. Green and Light Green: Filatura Di Crosa, Sympathie (50-gr., 150-yd. skein): 2 Forest Green #938, 1 Light Green #933.

Baby's Christening Gown, page 84, DMC Corporation, Cebelia, Size 30 (563-yd. ball): 1 White.

Soft Blocks, page 86, Orange: Coats & Clark, Red Heart Wintuck (114-gr., 253-yd. skein): 1 Mango #6023. Brunswick Yarns, Fore-'n-Aft Sport (50-gr., 175-yd. ball): 1 Canary #60083. Emu Yarns, Superwash DK (50-gr., 124-yd. ball): 1 Red #3051. Checkerboard: Emu Yarns, Superwash DK (50-gr., 124-yd. ball): 1 each Red #3051, Blue #3008. Brunswick Yarns, Fore-'n-Aft Sport (50-gr., 175-yd. ball): 1 Canary #60083. Pingouin, Pingofrance (50-gr., 150-yd. skein): 1 Kelly Green #176. Stripes: Brunswick Yarns, Fore-'n-Aft Sport (50-gr., 175-yd. ball): 1 each Blue Blaze #6042, White #6000, Canary #60083. Pingouin, Pingofrance (50-gr., 150-yd. skein): 1 Kelly Green #176.

Bonny Barrettes, page 89, DMC Corporation, Perle Cotton, Size 8 (95-yd. ball): 1 each White, Variegated Red #99, Black #310, Ecru, Peach #353.

Basket Lace, page 92, DMC Corporation, Cebelia, Size 30 (563-yd. ball): 2 Ecru. Madeira USA Inc., Supertwist #30 (1000m spool): 1 each Gold #24, Gold #25.

Miniature Quartet, page 96, Heart: DMC Corporation, Fil A Dentelles (100-yd. ball): 1 each Peach #754, Ecru. Pink Carnation: DMC Corporation, Fil A Dentelles (100-yd. ball): 1 Peach #754. Crowned Star: DMC Corporation, Fil A Dentelles (100-yd. ball): 1 Ecru. Peach Petals: DMC Corporation, Fil A Dentelles (100-yd. ball): 1 Peach #754.

Wrapped in Style, page 98, Pingouin, Berlingot (50-gr., 121-yd. ball): 8 Black #14. Marnel, Chi Chi Brilliant (50-gr., 98-yd. ball): 1 Black with Pink and Aqua #822. Berroco, Watercolor (50-gr., 125-yd. ball): 1 Black with Pink, Yellow, and Blue #261. Pingouin, Luciole (20-gr., 132-yd. ball): 1 Translucent with Gold and Turquoise #03.

Southwestern Tote Bag, page 101, Rowan Designer Collection, Cabled Mercerized Cotton (50-gr., 184-yd. ball): 4 Khaki #329; 1 each Lichen #327, Mushroom #325, Mauve #311. Plymouth Yarn Co., Bolo Fino (50-gr., 82-yd. ball): 1 each Turquoise #202, Rose #604.

Beaded Scarf, page 104, Caron Collection, Watercolours (40-yd. skein): 5 Slate.

Lacy Throw, page 106, Bucilla, Wondersheen (400-yd. ball): 36 Ecru.

TREATS & TRIBUTES

Patriotic Table Set, page 110, DMC Corporation, Cebelia Size 5, (141-yd. ball): 1 White. Aarlan, Cotonella (50-gr., 115-yd. ball): 1 each Blue #6207, Red #6205.

White Christmas, page 112, DMC Corporation, Perle Cotton, Size 5 (53-yd. ball): 30 White for tree skirt; 3 White for stocking.

Thanksgiving Plate Cover, page 118, Classic Elite Yarns, Newport (50-gr., 70-yd. skein): 2 Brown #2344; 1 each Green #3336, Gold #2341.

Easter Delights, page 120, Flower: DMC Corporation, Embroidery Floss (8-yd. skein): 2 Ecru; 1 each Medium Blue #341, Light Lavender #211, Shell Pink #818, Medium Lavender #340, Blue #809, Turquoise #964, Dark Purple #333. Butterfly: DMC Corporation, Embroidery Floss (8-yd. skein): 2 Ecru; 1 each Light Pink #689, Medium Pink #3354, Wine #315, Medium Purple #340, Dark Purple #333, Light Purple #341. Daffodil: DMC Corporation, Embroidery Floss (8-yd skein): 2 Ecru; 1 each Medium Green #912, Bright Yellow #727.

Holiday Trimmings, page 125, Tree: DMC Corporation, Coton Lustre Pour Tricot Brilliant (218-yd. ball): 3 Emerald #911. Peach and Green Sweater: Unger, Fluffy (50-gr., 156-yd. skein): Orange #583. Unger, Roly Sport (50-gr., 190-yd. skein): Light Green #4537. Gray Sweater: Filatura Di Crosa, Sympathie (50-gr., 150-yd. skein): Gray #932. Ivory Sweater: Brunswick Yarns, Pearl (50-gr., 110-yd. ball): Eggshell #59100. Berroco, Dante (50-gr., 90-yd. skein): Variegated Beige/Off-white/Taupe/Pale Blue #1093.

Jack-o'-lanterns, page 128, Emu Yarns, Superwash DK (50-gr. 124-yd. ball): 8 Dark Rust #3003, 5 Medium Rust #3014, 4 Coral #3055. Filatura Di Crosa, Sympathie (50-gr., 150-yd. skein): 2 Forest Green #938, 1 Green #934.

Poinsettia Throw, page 131, Aarlan, Swa Laine (50-gr. 105-yd. skein): 14 Forest Green #G1. Emu Yarns, Superwash DK (50-gr., 124-yd. ball): 1 Dark Red #3002.

Sparkling Ornaments, page 134, Icicles: DMC Corporation, Baroque (400-yd. ball): 1 White. Madeira USA Inc., Supertwist #30 (1000m spool): 1 each Silver Metallic #41, Silver Metallic #11. Garland: Madeira USA Inc., Supertwist #30 (1000m spool): 1 each Silver Metallic #41, Silver Metallic #11.

Yarn Sources

Aarlan
27452 Crestview Court
Farmington Hills, MI 48335

Berroco
Elmdale Road
P.O. Box 367
Uxbridge, MA 01569

Brunswick Yarns
P.O. Box 276
Pickens, SC 29671

Bucilla
230 Fifth Avenue
New York, NY 10001

Caron Collection
67 Poland Street
Bridgeport, CT 06605

Classic Elite Yarns
12 Perkins Street
Lowell, MA 01854

Coats & Clark
6900 South Point Drive
   North
Jacksonville, FL 32216

DMC Corporation
107 Trumbull Street
Elizabeth, NJ 07206

Emu Yarns
500 Lafayette Street
Bristol, PA 19007

Filatura Di Crosa
117 Dobbins Street
Brooklyn, NY 11222

Hayfield Yarns
204 Third Avenue South
Seattle, WA 98104

Kreinik Mfg. Co. Inc.
P.O. Box 1966
Parkersburg, WV 26102

Lane Borgosesia
128 Radio Circle
Mt. Kisco, NY 10549

Madeira USA Inc.
56 Primrose Drive
Oshea Industrial Park
Laconia, NH 03246

Marnel
no address available

Pingouin
P.O. Box 100
Highway 45
Jamestown, SC 29453

Plymouth Yarn Co.
500 Lafayette Street
Bristol, PA 19007

Rowan Designer
   Collection
5 North Boulevard
Amherst, NH 03031

Schewe
118 Ricardo Road
Mill Valley, CA 94941

Tahki Imports
11 Graphic Place
Moonachie, NJ 07074

Trendsetter Yarns
16742 Stagg Street, #107
Van Nuys, CA 91406

William Unger and
   Company
2478 East Main Street
Bridgeport, CT 06601